CW01500902

"A deep dive into the fascinating world of political esoterica, this
invigorating book will explain politicians to their voters and vice
versa – two groups who at times inhabit unparallel universes. All this
from the pen of Britain's doyen of political scientists, Philip Cowley,
and drawn from the pages of the MP's bible, The House *magazine."*
ANTHONY SELDON, HISTORIAN AND AUTHOR OF *THE IMPOSSIBLE*
OFFICE? THE HISTORY OF THE BRITISH PRIME MINISTER

"To just call Philip Cowley one of Britain's pre-eminent political
scientists – which he is – is to (almost) miss the point. The genius of
this tome is the way he combines cutting-edge academic insight with
an understanding of how the political system actually works and the
deepest dive around on the psychology of voters. Few academics have
grasped the central insight that sets Cowley apart – people are at
the heart of our political system, not structures, rules or history, and
this is what makes his work a joy. On top of this, combine his love
of trivia – only he would start a chapter analysing which motorway
service stations are in which constituencies – with a drive for
truth-seeking and myth-busting and you've got a rare commodity:
a political book that travels well beyond the smallest room in the
house. A serious work that everyone should enjoy."
SAM COATES, DEPUTY POLITICAL EDITOR, SKY NEWS

"More entertaining than it has any right to
be and absurdly full of nerdy fun facts."
MARIE LE CONTE, JOURNALIST AND AUTHOR OF *HONOURABLE*
MISFITS: A BRIEF HISTORY OF BRITAIN'S WEIRDEST,
UNLUCKIEST AND MOST OUTRAGEOUS MPs

PHILIP COWLEY

THE SMALLEST ROOM IN THE HOUSE

50 POLITICAL ODDITIES TO READ IN MORE THAN ONE SITTING

Biteback Publishing

First published in Great Britain in 2025 by
Biteback Publishing Ltd, London
Copyright © Philip Cowley 2025

Illustrations © Tracy Worrall.

ISBN 978-1-78590-970-2

10 9 8 7 6 5 4 3 2 1

A CIP catalogue record for this book is available from the British Library.

Set in Minion Pro and Century Gothic Pro

Printed and bound in Great Britain by
CPI Group (UK) Ltd, Croydon CR0 4YY

FSC
www.fsc.org
MIX
Paper | Supporting
responsible forestry
FSC® C013604

This one's for Maggie

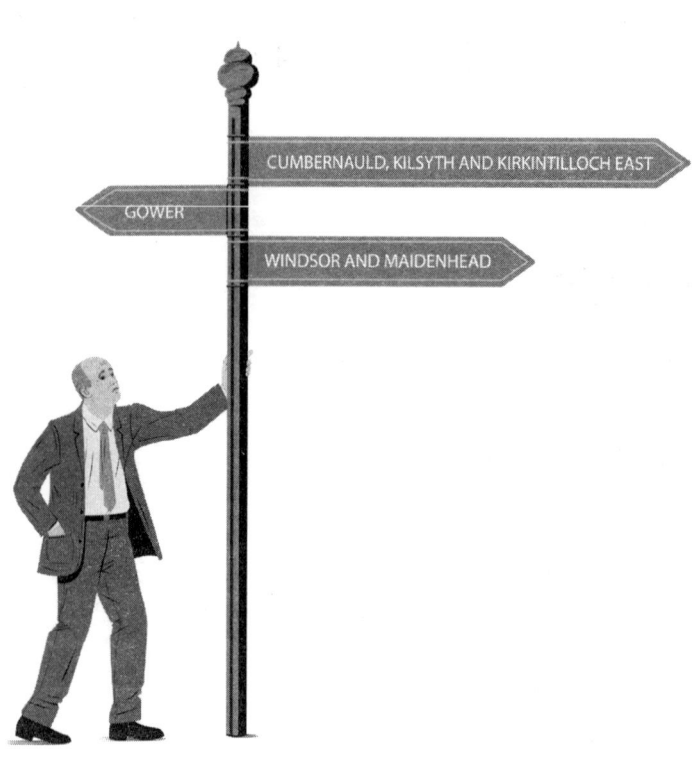

CONTENTS

Introduction   ix

Chapter 1   Trust   1

Chapter 2   Chips   7

Chapter 3   Dullards   13

Chapter 4   +/-3   19

Chapter 5   Riots   25

Chapter 6   Beards   31

Chapter 7   Graduates   37

Chapter 8   Fights   43

Chapter 9   Preferences   49

Chapter 10   Newbies   53

Chapter 11   Projection   59

Chapter 12   Lawns   65

Chapter 13   Winners   71

Chapter 14   Potholes   77

Chapter 15   Obviously   83

Chapter 16	Roles	89
Chapter 17	Pledges	95
Chapter 18	Flats	101
Chapter 19	Realism	107
Chapter 20	Loadsamoney	113
Chapter 21	Presence	119
Chapter 22	Leaflets	125
Chapter 23	Data	131
Chapter 24	Scum	137
Chapter 25	Whatever	143
Chapter 26	Visits	147
Chapter 27	PMQs	151
Chapter 28	And	157
Chapter 29	PMs	163
Chapter 30	By-elections	169
Chapter 31	Whoops	175
Chapter 32	Inbetweeners	179
Chapter 33	Rebels	185
Chapter 34	Locks	189
Chapter 35	Locals	195
Chapter 36	Fakes	201
Chapter 37	Cockroaches	207
Chapter 38	Boots	213
Chapter 39	Dissent	219
Chapter 40	Predictions	225
Chapter 41	Letters	229

Chapter 42   Curvilinear   235

Chapter 43   Ishoos   241

Chapter 44   Splits   247

Chapter 45   N   253

Chapter 46   Bats   257

Chapter 47   Majorities   263

Chapter 48   Apps   269

Chapter 49   Teaching   275

Chapter 50   Quotes   281

About the Author   287

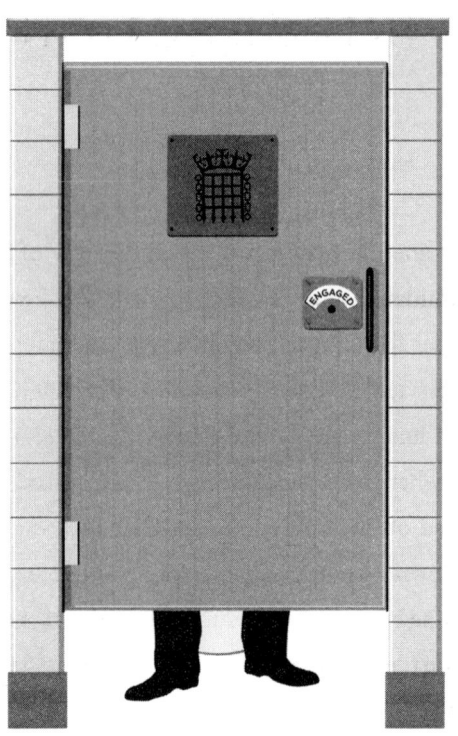

INTRODUCTION

People sometimes complain that the Palace of Westminster is intimidating and difficult to navigate. Just be grateful that it's better than it used to be. Back in the 1990s, when I was there to interview MPs as a postgraduate student, I used to take in a packed lunch in my briefcase, and because there was then literally nowhere for visitors to eat, I would head to the gents toilet located off the Lower Waiting Hall, lock myself in a WC and wolf down a couple of sandwiches, as quickly as possible, before anyone began to wonder what exactly was going on in the cubicle. Don't let anyone tell you that academic field work isn't glamorous.

Despite a long-standing fascination with politics, I had realised in early adulthood that I would – for multiple reasons, most of them not to my credit – make a truly terrible politician. But if I couldn't *do* it, maybe I could at least study it, teach it or write about it. Inexplicably, lunch on the khazi wasn't enough to deter me – and I would spend much of the next thirty or so years knocking around the Houses of Parliament as part of various research projects; equally inexplicably (or so it would have seemed to me when I was locked in the loo), people did indeed begin to ask me to write about the subject.

Most of the fifty chapters in this book began life as a column in *The House*, Parliament's fortnightly in-house magazine, which is sent to British MPs and peers. The column started in 2023 with the slightly pompous title 'The Professor Will See You Now'. We called it that because we couldn't think of anything better, even if it does sound a bit like a sexual harassment case waiting to happen. For all its flaws, the title did at least capture the basic idea behind the articles: I would take some topical, relevant or otherwise interesting piece of academic work on politics that had been published recently and try to explain it to the magazine's readership.

'You'll run out of stuff to discuss,' predicted a more cynical colleague as soon as the first column appeared. Thankfully, the problem was the opposite, and what was originally going to be an occasional column became a regular feature. About twenty articles in, it occurred to both me and the editor that there was probably a book in it. Here it is.

'It'll make a great loo book,' declared James at Biteback – and while this might have dented my *amour propre* a little, he was right, as always. This is not a book to be read in one sitting. There's no pretension here to any overarching theme. This isn't like one of those books you see on the business shelf in

WHSmith at Heathrow: *Six Lessons That Will Change the Way You See the World*. Or even one of those *50 Objects That Explain Britain* tomes. An honest subtitle would be something like *Random Stuff That Interested the Author When His Deadline Was Approaching*. These are just fifty topics that seemed interesting to me when I sat down to write and I thought might be interesting to readers of the magazine – and now, with luck, to you. If you get through more than two chapters per visit then you need to eat more prunes.

The column was a pleasure to produce. The editors allowed me to focus on almost anything I wanted. I religiously stuck to the brief to publicise recent academic material (I use the word 'recently' thirty-one times in what follows), except on the many occasions when I didn't. And the definition of 'recent' got stretched somewhat; several of the pieces I ended up discussing were published before I was born.

I took a series of early editorial decisions. None of the pieces of academic work discussed would be by me; I broke that rule in the very first article and on multiple occasions thereafter. I also decided at the outset that I would not use the column to criticise or slag off other people's work. This seemed unfair, given that they had no right of reply, and also not in the collective good. The aim was to try to promote the many excellent academic studies that are regularly published on politics and which deserved a wider audience. If I didn't think some piece of research was solid, I just wouldn't talk about it. That rule I did stick to, even if I sailed close to the wind on a few occasions. But for the most part, I saw the column as a chance to publicise the sort of research that, despite its quality, sits unread (or if not unread then maybe under-read?) in academic journals.

The choice of subject matter was determined mostly by the stuff I liked – which means a lot of process and not a lot of policy – but also with an eye to the sort of things I thought MPs might be interested in, which means there's a lot in here on Parliament and elections. If it's not discussed here, that doesn't mean it's not important; it just means that I didn't write about it. There is, for example, nothing in here on how we cure life-threatening diseases or bring about world peace; that doesn't mean I wouldn't value them.

The original articles in *The House* mostly ran to about 600 words. I've taken the opportunity of this book to expand each piece slightly, often including material that had ended up on the cutting-room floor. I've also updated some of the articles in the process and occasionally corrected errors that had been spotted by eagle-eyed readers. None of the chapters is identical to the article originally published. Equally, though, none of them is all that different. They remain very short essays, offering snapshots into the issues discussed. If you want more, there is a brief further reading section at the end of each chapter.

Nine of the chapters began life elsewhere, albeit in a very different form. But the rest are all from *The House*. From the beginning, I've been grateful for all the team there for their support.

Rosa Prince took a punt on the original idea and Alan White, Francis Elliott and Sally Dawson edited with charm and style.

Rereading en masse what were originally separate and ephemeral pieces brings your stylistic foibles into sharp focus. Too much Latin. Too much Wodehouse. I've tried to tone both down here. I use some words far too frequently; 'fascinating' is an obvious weakness of mine. And the effects of having had two born-again grandparents – one ran a Christian bookshop and the other would spend his spare time pounding the streets of Newquay proselytising – came through in the number of biblical references I realised I use. (At one point, I had made the same joke about John the Baptist twice.) So again, I have toned that down a little.

Those same grandparents would, however, have been *horrified* by the various rude words that have crept in. When I am on my deathbed and my grandchildren ask me what I am most proud of in life, I will summon up all my remaining energy, pull them close and whisper in their ears: 'I got the Scunthorpe gag in Chapter 26 into *The House* magazine.'

CHAPTER 1

TRUST

The latest data on the level of trust in various professions makes salutary reading for the political class. In the most recent Ipsos poll, for example, just 18 per cent of people said they trusted politicians to tell the truth. Of the twenty-six professions about which the survey asked, politicians came bottom.

Actually, that's not true. The 18 per cent figure is from when the survey was first conducted in 1983. More than forty years ago – before anyone had heard of sleaze, or Iraq, or MPs' expenses, or Covid or whatever else has been used to explain our lack of trust in politicians – MPs were already down there with estate agents and journalists.

Since then, the veracity score for politicians has gone as high as 23 per cent, which isn't very high, and as low as 9 per cent, which is very low. The figure from the most recent poll, last year, was 11 per cent.

The figure for government ministers is only slightly higher, at 15 per cent. For reasons I have never really understood, when this question was first asked, ministers polled worse than politicians in general. From 2000 onwards, ministers polled better than politicians. Answers on a postcard, please.

The same poll, by the way, finds that 85 per cent think professors are trustworthy – a figure that only leads me to conclude most people haven't actually met a professor.

This is not to say that there isn't a problem with trust in politicians or engagement with politics – but it is one reason why it is best to be wary of politicians who talk of their desire to regain the trust of the British people. You can't regain something you never had in the first place.

Still, just because things were bad before doesn't mean they are not getting worse – as demonstrated by my hairline. Some new research, just published in the *British Journal of Political Science*, attempts to test this systematically. It examined levels of trust in three representative institutions – Parliament, government and political parties – along with three of what they term 'implementing' institutions – the civil service, the legal system and the police. It draws on data from almost 3,400 separate surveys across 143 countries between 1958 and 2019. That's more than 5 million data points. It's the sort of big data research that makes us lesser mortals feel inadequate.

The stats are quite complicated – they use Bayesian dynamic latent trait models, if you are interested – but the overall findings are not. There is clear evidence of a decline in trust in representative institutions across the world. Trust in parliaments, for example, has gone down by around 9 percentage points in democracies between 1990 and 2019.

By contrast, trust in implementing organisations has remained pretty constant or even gone upwards. Over that same time period, trust in the police, for example, has trended upwards by about 13 percentage points. That is presumably because there are never any scandals involving the police.

It's a fascinating paper, packed with findings; the online appendices include 142 pages of supplementary information. If you've ever wondered whether people in Lithuania have become more or less trusting of the police since 1990, then this is the research for you. (Spoiler: the answer is more.)

These trends are not uniform. There are countries in which trust in, say, their parliament has stayed broadly the same. But the level of trust has risen in just six democracies, of which the most populous is Ecuador (population: < 20 million). The trends are also not linear. This means that in any one country, at any one point in time, it might look as if what is happening is just trendless fluctuation. But seen en masse like this, the global patterns become more obvious.

This presents an interesting challenge. Do you, as an academic or practitioner, look at the fact that some countries have bucked the trends and say to yourself, channelling Jim Carrey in *Dumb and Dumber*, 'You're telling me there's a chance?' Or do you accept that you are on the wrong side of a global wave of discontent and there's probably not a lot you can do about it?

What of the UK? Here, things are perhaps not quite what you might expect. For one thing, the research reveals no long-term decline in trust in the three implementing organisations. Trust in the police, for example, had been falling but is now back to roughly the same levels as in 1990. Ditto for trust in political parties, which seems basically unchanged.

The authors report trust in government in the UK to have fallen but describe the situation with trust in Westminster as 'borderline'. As my grandmother used to say, thank heaven for small mercies.

'Borderline', just to be clear, is on the downside – that is, somewhere between trust being constant and trust falling – rather than on the upside. Digging into the data a bit more, it looks as if trust in both Parliament and government in the UK have slightly declined over the last thirty or so years. In one case (government), it's fallen by a difference that is statistically significant, and in the other (Parliament), by an amount that just fails to make statistical significance, hence the borderline. But the substantive effects are pretty similar.

It's probably best not to be too celebratory about it. For one thing, this research was looking at trends, not absolute levels. As the data at the start of the chapter indicated, trust in politicians in the UK was already pretty low; it didn't have all that far to fall. And it is now being classed as borderline. No one has ever thrown a party to celebrate being borderline.

4

Further reading

V. Valgarðsson et al., 'A Crisis of Political Trust? Global Trends in Institutional Trust from 1958 to 2019', *British Journal of Political Science* (2025).

CHAPTER 2

CHIPS

Did you know that none of the motorway service stations along the M4 is in a Conservative-held constituency? From Pont Abraham in Carmarthenshire to Heston in West London ('Only a fool would stop at Heston,' as Nessa says in *Gavin & Stacey*), all eleven service stations are in either Labour or Lib Dem seats. You might well respond that I need to get out more, but then it was getting out more that got me here in the first place. I sat the other day having a break at Leigh Delamere, wondering both what constituency I was in and how it ever became legal to charge that much for a cup of coffee.

Or take football grounds, something else I've been tracking for a while. After 2019, Premier League grounds were overwhelmingly in Labour-held constituencies that voted Remain. Once you dropped into the Championship, the Labour dominance continued, but with the majority of grounds in Leave-voting constituencies. By League One, the Labour dominance had gone and grounds were mainly in Leave-voting seats. This remained true for League Two and the National League. In the Premier League, 75 per cent of clubs were found in Labour-held seats; by time you got to the National League, the figure was just 25 per cent. In the Premier League, 70 per cent of grounds were in Remain-voting constituencies; in the National League, 67 per cent were in Leave-voting constituencies.

Just in case it's not blindingly obvious, the causal link here is not that voting Labour or Remain causes your football team to get better, but rather that Premier League clubs are mostly in big cities and big cities largely voted Remain and (even in 2019) return Labour MPs. As you move down the leagues, you get smaller cities and towns, which are more likely to be Conservative and/or Leave-voting.

In England and Wales, at least, things got a lot easier to explain after 2024, because there was just one football league club in a Conservative-held constituency (Bromley, if you're interested). Barnet's return to the football league in 2025 made it two. That's also quite revealing in its own way. You have to dip into non-league football before things get a bit more varied, as they now are in Scotland.

In a similar vein, a switched-on Labour MP once told me that UKIP, as then was, did well in places where you could get good fish and chips. I nodded politely at the time, but a new research paper published in the journal *Geoforum* has tested something similar, examining the relationship between the prevalence of fish and chip shops in an area and voting patterns in the 2016

Brexit referendum, and it turns out that Labour MP was on to something.

You have to love research in which someone has written 'no study has examined the relationship between Brexit and fish and chips' – it's reminiscent of that bit in *Lucky Jim* in which Dixon ponders the phrase 'considering this strangely neglected topic' – and where the researchers have downloaded a database of restaurants from yell.com, where there are, just like Heinz, fifty-seven varieties. But, like football grounds or service stations, it turns out chip shops offer a good insight into electoral geography.

The most common food outlets in the UK are generic fast-food places; next comes Indian restaurants, with fish and chip shops or restaurants in third. Chippies are not the main type of outlet in any London constituency; the paper contains some fascinating maps, including one of London that shows Italian restaurants predominate in the centre, surrounded by a ring of constituencies where generic takeaways dominate, and then an outer ring of constituencies where Indian restaurants are the most common, a bit like the M25 circling London. (Three of the four service stations on the M25 are in Conservative-held seats, in case you were wondering.)

But chippies dominate elsewhere outside of the capital – along various bits of the south coast, around Cardiff, on the edges of the central belt in Scotland – and the researchers identify a 'fish and chip wall' of English constituencies, a contiguous area running from Southport to Scarborough to Whitby, where the chip shop is king.

In Yorkshire and the Humber, the region where they are most common, chip shops make up a fifth of all restaurants. Here, the Leave share of the vote was 58 per cent. In London, where chippies make up under 8 per cent of restaurants, the Leave share was 40 per cent. A more sophisticated analysis finds that the relationship holds at constituency level: the greater the preponderance of chip shops, the higher the Leave vote.

A secondary analysis compares the Brexit vote with a measure of restaurant diversity. It finds the opposite effect: the Leave vote share goes down as restaurants become more diverse. Ditto for a separate test for Japanese restaurants. The authors' surnames are Pickering and Tanaka, if you were wondering about their choices of cuisines to test.

What's interesting here, though, is that the chip shop isn't just a proxy for other, easily controlled, variables. The chip-shop effect remains, even after controlling for other demographics. Restaurants, the authors note, are 'behavioural proxies', which reflect broader cultural and political contexts. We are what we eat.

A coda: if cuisine isn't your thing, another new research paper, just published in *Political Studies*, examines the effects of social mobility on the Brexit vote. Living in an area on the up, compared to one that wasn't, was associated with almost 7 percentage points difference in the Leave vote in 2016. This effect held regardless of one's own social mobility. As the researchers write: 'Individuals see how neighbours, colleagues, family members and friends, who tend to live in close vicinity, fare.' They vote according to how the people surrounding them are faring, not how socially mobile they have been. We are also where we live.

Further reading

A. McNeil and P. Sturgis, 'Does Local Area Social Mobility Affect Political Alienation?', *Political Studies* (2024).

S. Pickering and S. Tanaka, 'A taste for deprivation? Fish, chips and leaving the European Union', *Geoforum* (2025).

CHAPTER 3

DULLARDS

'Why don't you write something about that study that found Leave voters were less intelligent than Remain voters?' said someone who, up until that point, I had always considered to be a friend.

It's such an incendiary topic that my initial view was that it would be more pleasant to cover my genitals with honey before sticking them in a beehive. But on reflection, maybe it's a useful exercise, because of the finding itself but also because of what it tells you about how to interpret these sorts of studies.

To summarise: the research asked people to complete five tests of cognitive ability, measuring reasoning, fluency and so on. How many words could they recall from a list? How many animals could they name in a minute? How good was their subtraction? Could they fill in the blank in a sequence of numbers? How was their numerical reasoning?

On average, those who voted Remain scored higher on these measures than those who voted Leave. Plus, as cognitive ability scores increased, so did the likelihood of voting Remain. Of those whose cognitive ability scores put them in the bottom 10 per cent, some 40 per cent voted Remain; for those in the top decile, the figure was about 73 per cent.

The dataset consisted of around 6,000 individuals from 3,000 or so couples. Researchers found that while most couples voted the same way, in the 14 per cent of cases where there was intra-couple disharmony, the higher-scoring partner was more likely to have voted Remain. This last finding is especially interesting, because couples will for the most part be exposed to the same environment and external stimuli – and because, in the words of the paper, 'in the spirit of assortative mating, individuals within couples are likely to be similar to each other in other observable ways'.

A useful first question to ask is whether a study seems pukka. This one drew on the well-established Understanding Society survey, a nationally representative and large-scale survey carried out each year. It wasn't based on six people the authors met down the pub. Plus, it appeared in a peer-reviewed outlet – that is, one in which the work was read by other experts in the field before publication. Peer review is absolutely not a guarantee of quality – some shockers do occasionally sneak through – but it's still useful at filtering out obviously flawed studies.

None of that means we should treat the findings as gospel, but it does mean we can at least give them some credibility. As part of that process, for example, you might expect reviewers to consider whether the study had considered other factors that might be explaining the results, and indeed they had.

Second, always ask yourself: is this at least plausible? Here (and at the risk of getting bombarded with hate mail) the answer is yes, not least because it's not the only study to have claimed to have found this effect. We know both age and education are important factors in determining attitudes towards Brexit, and cognitive functions decline with age while increasing with educational attainment. (For the avoidance of doubt, while education and intelligence are not the same – as anyone working in a university is painfully aware – they are not entirely unrelated either.) Given all this, it would, I think, be surprising if there weren't *some* differences in cognitive functions between Leavers and Remainers.

This particular piece of research claims to have found something more than this, however – that is, differences in cognitive functions above and beyond those you would expect based on other demographics. But the core finding is perhaps not all that surprising.

Yet the key thing with research papers like this is always to consider the size of the difference and to remember that such findings are almost always probabilistic, not absolutes. If I told you that nine-year-olds are taller on average than eight-year-olds, a) no one would be shocked and b) no one would think I was claiming that *all* nine-year-olds were taller than *all* eight-year-olds. This is obvious when dealing with something prosaic like height but always seems to get overlooked when discussing anything more controversial, like politics.

This research isn't claiming that all Leavers had low levels of cognitive ability or that all Remainers shone. In fact, the research paper itself is clear about the fact that there are significant overlaps between the two groups. Just over a third of Leave voters, for example, had higher cognitive ability than the average Remain voter. There were plenty of sharp Leavers and plenty of dullard Remainers.

Or take the intra-couple differences. Where they disagreed, the highest-scoring one was about 10 per cent more likely to vote Remain. That's a non-trivial effect, but it still means there were lots of couples where the Leaver was the bright spark and the Remainer was a bit slower on the uptake.

I don't, for the record, especially like the way the paper is framed, with this higher average level of cognitive ability enabling brighter Remainers to see through the Leave campaign's more dodgy claims. Yes, it's true that people with higher cognitive functions are more likely to be able to see through misinformation (although, again, this is relative – lots of supposedly clever people fall for misinformation all the time), but this implies that only one side in the Brexit referendum made dubious claims, which is a curious way to remember the events of 2016.

I also struggle slightly with the normative implications. It's an interesting finding, but so what? This sort of study seems to appeal to a certain type of passionate Remainer who struggles with the fact that they lost the referendum and is always looking for other people to blame. Successful politicians work with the electorate they are given, not the one they wished they had.

Regardless, the research itself looks kosher. Now, where's that beehive?

Further reading

C. Dawson and P. Baker, 'Cognitive ability and voting behaviour in the 2016 UK referendum on European Union membership', *PLoS ONE* (2023).

CHAPTER 4

+ / - 3

Every election, the optimist in me hopes that it will be a contest in which opinion polls are properly reported. The pessimist in me knows that pollsters and journalists need the cash and clicks that come with overhyping poll findings.

Most informed observers – readers of this book, say – know that opinion polls come with uncertainty built in. For most standard opinion polls in the UK, the margin of error (MoE) is plus or minus 3 percentage points. In other words, if a poll puts a party on 40 per cent, it means their actual level of support is somewhere between 37 and 43 per cent. Its scale may vary occasionally (and it's slightly more complicated than this simplified version makes out), but MoE is an ever-present fact of polling life.

The consequences of it are often less understood. When comparing changes over time, the uncertainty applies to both the current and the past figure. To take a recent example, after the 2023 Autumn Statement, *The Times* reported that according to YouGov, Conservative support had risen by 4 points compared to the last poll by the same company. Pre-statement, the Conservatives were on 21 per cent; afterwards, they polled 25 per cent. That could have been a 4-point jump in support as a favourable reaction to the policies announced, which is how it got written up. But that 4-point poll increase would also be perfectly consistent with actual support for the Conservatives having been stable at 22, 23, or 24 per cent – or even having fallen slightly (24 per cent before, 22 per cent after). And indeed, once a few more polls were published, that more sober assessment seemed to be correct. Any apparent bounce from the Autumn Statement vanished and Conservative spirits sank again.

Just to be clear, we don't know that the Autumn Statement didn't stir something in voters' hearts. Perhaps they reacted favourably to it, but then before the next opinion poll was published, something else came along to make them less positive about the government and Conservative support went back to its original level. It's a possible explanation of what went on. My view (and, I think, that of most who study polls) is that it is more likely that the apparent jump in Tory support was a mirage, probably caused by the pre-statement poll, at 21 per cent, being on the low side for Conservative support at the time and the post-statement poll essentially just being a return to the norm. Either way, the important point here is that it would have been better not to have written it up as something significant and exciting, given that it could plausibly have been just noise.

It is not just that this slightly hysterical reporting is misleading. There is growing evidence that it can also be consequential. A recent piece of research tested British voters' reactions to these apparent changes in party support. In a series of polling experiments, voters were shown one set of poll figures and asked how likely it was that the party in the lead would win. Another group were shown the same figures but this time including the degree of change since the last poll (+3, +6 or whatever). Do that and you discover that voters are responsive to momentum. If a party's support had increased since the last poll, it was seen as more likely to win, compared to when voters were shown the same poll figures without any indication of the direction of travel.

Unsurprisingly, the larger the momentum, the bigger the effect – but the effect held even if the change made little difference to a party's chances of victory and, crucially, even if the change was within the margin of error. Even if the changes in the level of support could have been entirely due to a random polling error, telling people about them altered the way that they interpreted the poll – and how they saw the nature of the political race. Parties could appear to have the Big Mo, even when it was really just MoE.

A second recent study tested this directly. A neat survey experiment in Germany showed people opinion polls both with and without the margins of error and compared their reactions. The point estimates (38 per cent, say) seem definitive – more definitive than they actually are – but once you present voters with the uncertainty inherent in polling (35–41 per cent), it turns out they interpret things differently. The uncertainty changes their tactical considerations. In particular, the study found that if the margin of error makes the race look close and uncertain, voters become more likely to vote for one of the major parties.

This is all why it is never sensible to get too excited about any individual poll results. Instead, we need to look for wider trends. It is also why it is important that news outlets and others report polls properly. The German study showed that how the polls were reported was a significant factor in voters' interpretations. Perhaps understandably, voters find MoE tricky to understand. Just saying that stats have a +/-3 per cent MoE – which is what most British media organisations do, albeit often in the small print – isn't as significant as the way the outlets interpret the results.

To return to the *Times* article, the print edition headline talked of the Autumn Statement having been 'a surprise vote winner'; the online version said it gave the Tories 'a bump in the polls'. The article began: 'Rishi Sunak received a four-point poll boost last night as voters broadly welcomed the tax cuts in Jeremy Hunt's autumn statement'. Winner. Bump. Boost. Well, maybe. But, as it turned out, probably not.

Further reading

M. Barnfield, 'Momentum in the polls raises electoral expectations', *Electoral Studies* (2023).

W. Krause and C. Gahn, 'Should we include margins of error in public opinion polls?', *European Journal of Political Research* (2023).

CHAPTER 5

RIOTS

We would be worried about the probity of any general election that witnessed thirty-nine riots and a further 300 or so further violent incidents, resulting in seventeen deaths.

Yet that was the scorecard for the general election of 1868, just in England and Wales. One riot in Newport took place over multiple days and involved the military being called out; a woman and her child died from bayonet wounds. The military were also involved in quelling riots in Blaenavon, Boston, Bolton and Wakefield. In Barnsley, there was no need for the army because the police used cutlasses.

It wasn't a one-off either. The two elections that followed the introduction of the secret ballot in 1872 saw a further sixty-one riots and 400 or so other violent incidents between them, plus another thirteen deaths.

As late as the election of 1885, there were twenty-seven riots, over 360 incidents and five deaths. These, in the words of the *Saturday Review*, included 'deliberate attempts to murder unpopular candidates'. *The Times* described that election as 'on the whole, pure', which makes you wonder what the impure ones looked like.

These statistics are all taken from a fascinating new article, just published in *Past and Present*, which comprehensively demonstrates that historians have hugely underestimated the scale of the violence involved in Victorian elections. The process of democratisation in Britain after 1832 was not as placid as it is often claimed. Indeed, rather than declining as the nineteenth century wore on, there was a sharp increase in the levels of electoral violence between the Second and Third Reform Acts.

There were some regional variations (East Anglia and the East Midlands seem to have been particularly dangerous places to stand for Parliament), but it was pretty common everywhere. In the fifty or so years between 1832 and 1880, over 90 per cent of constituencies saw some electoral violence. The authors concluded that violence was 'endemic' in nineteenth-century elections.

Not only had historians previously underestimated its frequency but they also misunderstood its nature. What violence did occur in nineteenth-century elections had been seen as spontaneous bottom-up rowdiness, which elites often did their best to subdue. But there is, according to this new research, pretty clear evidence that much of it was in fact coordinated by politicians, who used it as a campaigning tool.

Violence was more commonly found in marginal seats and often involved 'roughs', one of the phrases used at the time, although they also went by other fairly self-descriptive labels, such as bludgeon-men, toughs, thugs and so on. They would be hired to break up rival meetings or intimidate voters. In response, parties would also hire defensive roughs – 'watchers', 'protection men' or 'doorkeepers'. This wasn't just ritualistic violence or evidence of discontent; it was strategic. Overall, the authors estimate that 'roughs' were involved in about 40 per cent of the election riots they identified.

Things only began to calm down after 1886, albeit with what the paper calls a 'modest bounce' in the first election of 1910 (a modest bounce in which 20 per cent of constituencies saw some violence). The authors note that even full-on riots, involving military interventions and deaths, often failed to become front-page news at the time and could be found be tucked away on the inside pages of newspapers. This is a commentary on their unexceptional nature but also perhaps excuses the inability of previous historians to identify them. Only two English counties didn't experience at least one election riot between 1832 and 1914 – and in Lancashire alone, for example, there were twenty-six.

Here's four examples of the sort of stuff they identified, taken more or less at random:

- In 1841 in Dover, during the nomination process, a crowd assaulted one of the candidates. Military reinforcements were required and the Riot Act was read.
- After the close of poll in Newbury in 1868, a crowd of 150

or so people assaulted Conservative supporters and damaged property, including the Conservative committee room.

- In 1886, a Unionist meeting in Lincoln was stormed; fists and furniture were thrown.
- In Derbyshire in January 1910, two farmers were assaulted as they returned from voting.

Those four examples include one each of the authors' four types of electoral violence: individuals, incidents, disturbances, riots.

As always, no doubt a different coding scheme would come up with different figures. One man's riot might be another's violent disturbance – although in many cases, like the one discussed, these riots involved the reading of the Riot Act, so there's not really much to debate. It's also difficult to argue that much with the number of deaths. Slice it how you like, the sheer scale of violent incidents is so great that the overall conclusion seems unquestionable.

This research was only possible because of the mass digitisation of newspaper archives – which remain a criminally under-utilised resource. Using machine learning but checked by a team of research assistants, the authors searched for examples of electoral violence in over 1.3 million articles in the British Newspaper Archive, covering more than 1,000 local and national papers.

Despite excluding Scotland (on grounds of cost) and Ireland (where levels of violence were already known to be relatively high), the results still involved a corpus of some 2 billion words. It is research that would simply not have been possible without digitisation; historians, the authors of this research argue, 'have underestimated what they have been unable to quantify'.

Further reading

L. Blaxill et al., 'Electoral Violence in England and Wales, 1832–1914', *Past and Present* (2024). The project has an accompanying interactive map at https://victorianelectionviolence.uk/interactive-map, which allows you to examine the details of 3,000 separate incidents.

CHAPTER 6

BEARDS

Lather up! As the 2024 election approached, bearded Conservative MPs were said to be reaching for the razors, in the belief that facial fungus was a turn-off for the voters. 'I've lost count of the number of times people have said voters are less likely to back you if you have a beard,' one Tory MP apparently told the *Sun on Sunday*.

This story is a hardy perennial of British election coverage, reappearing periodically through the decades whenever MPs or journalists have become particularly desperate, for votes or copy respectively.

Back in 1966, a Liberal council candidate was told to shave because a beard didn't match his party's image – which, if nothing else, does go to show how party images can change over time. At the turn of the century, it was Frank Dobson – named Beard 2000 by the Beard Liberation Front – who was advised by Labour strategists that sacrificing his beard would help his campaign to become Mayor of London. In the words of the *Guardian* article on the story: 'It would reveal the party's candidate as a reinvigorated figure … [and] make him more appealing to women and younger voters.' Dobson declined, declaring: 'If it's good enough for Abe Lincoln, it's good enough for me.' As the paper noted, a cynic might wonder if the idea had been floated solely to enable Dobson to demonstrate his independence by telling the party advisers where to stick the idea.

On the face of it (no pun intended), the idea that a candidate's appearance might matter is not entirely ridiculous. There is plenty of evidence that voters, especially those with relatively low levels of interest in politics, make decisions based on intellectual shortcuts, known in the trade as 'heuristics'. Appearance is a well-utilised heuristic in life – what is often referred to as 'the pretty premium'. It would be strange if it didn't impact how people viewed politicians.

There is indeed research showing that the more attractive candidates tend to win British elections. A study of the 2010 election found that in close races, attractiveness alone successfully predicted the outcomes of almost three-quarters of contests. It's a very similar figure to that in the US, where researchers found that almost 70 per cent of Congressional races could be predicted from the candidates' looks. It's a remarkable finding for many reasons – and not just because if the House of Commons is made up of the more attractive candidates, can you imagine what the losers must have looked like?

I appreciate this joke is a bit rich coming from an academic, not all of whom are renowned for their movie-star looks. If politics is, as it is often described, show business for ugly people, then what must that say about those who study it?

When it comes to beards specifically, there is lots of research showing that people make assumptions about people with facial hair. One US study found that politicians with beards were seen as more masculine and more competent but less supportive of feminist issues – and less likely to be supported by feminists. That these judgements were not accurate – bearded Congressmen had essentially the same voting records as the clean-shaven – is irrelevant.

Similarly, in 2017, a male grooming brand in the UK released a poll claiming that almost 70 per cent of us did not like male politicians with facial hair. Roughly the same percentage thought a clean-shaven politician was more trustworthy and more professional. In both the US and UK studies, women were marginally more pogonophobic.

Yet consider these cautionary notes. Studies like these sometimes test one variable – in this case, appearance – in isolation. It is therefore very much a maximal finding, at the top end of any estimates. A real politician's looks are in the mix along with their record, their views and their party. The actual electorate consists of people who would vote for your party even if you looked like Quasimodo, others who won't no matter how good looking you are and many others who don't know what you look like anyway. Even more sophisticated studies, which test multiple characteristics, aren't testing everything that might be out there in the real world.

Plus, things like attractiveness are context-specific, changing over time and place. The US study on beards, for example, drew on the views of students from a Midwest university. How sure are we that what floated their boats will be similar to the things that might win the approval of a pensioner in Yorkshire?

And even if we accept the premise, think about some of the numbers involved. In Westminster elections, the personal vote of an incumbent MP is worth a couple of percentage points. We don't know the exact composition of that (how much is a reputation for good constituency service worth, for example, compared to your voting record?), but the proportion of votes resulting from appearance must be a fraction, and probably just a small fraction, of that. And then consider how many beards there are to lose in the first place. We can exclude the women and most of the men are clean-shaven already.

So, we end up talking about an effect of a fraction of a percentage point in a handful of seats.

But this is easy for me to say. It's not my job on the line. If I was a shaggy MP, in a potentially marginal seat, I would be very aware that that fraction might matter. Every little helps, as the ad puts it. I wouldn't want to wake up the day after polling with a magnificent beard but no job. Maybe I would still reach for the razor.

Further reading

R. Herrick et al., 'Razor's Edge: The Politics of Facial Hair', *Social Science Quarterly* (2015).

K. Mattes and C. Milazzo, 'Pretty faces, marginal races: Predicting election outcomes using trait assessments of British parliamentary candidates', *Electoral Studies* (2014).

CHAPTER 7

GRADUATES

When Margaret Thatcher achieved her second landslide in 1987, seven in ten voters had finished their education aged sixteen or younger. Those with no formal qualifications made up 40 per cent of the electorate, outnumbering university graduates by more than five to one.

Fast forward thirty years to 2017, and the voters that Theresa May faced – with somewhat less success – looked rather different. Nearly a quarter had a degree, a group now more numerous than the unqualified. The tipping point came at the end of the New Labour era. Before 2010, graduates were outnumbered, often massively, by those without qualifications. From 2010 onwards, graduates outnumbered the unqualified.

In their excellent book *Brexitland* (from where I have cheerfully lifted these figures), Maria Sobolewska and Rob Ford identify the growth in education as one of the biggest changes in the composition of the electorate over the past forty years.

When graduates made up such a tiny proportion of the

electorate, no one really cared that much about their political behaviour. Early election studies paid relatively little attention to higher education as a factor that might influence someone's vote.

But as their numbers have grown – and continue to grow – they have become more important, a process that has been magnified by education becoming a more significant cleavage among the electorate, as a result of the Brexit referendum and the Brexit-suffused elections that followed, where education was a clear divide. In 2015, the difference between the Conservatives' lead among graduates and the rest of the population was never larger than 7 percentage points. In 2019, by contrast, Labour enjoyed a small lead among graduate voters, despite trailing by more than 20 percentage points among the rest of the population.

Some of this is the result of age. Following the post-1992 expansion of universities, graduates are on average still a younger segment of the population. But this doesn't explain all of it, because graduates have long been known to be, on average, more liberal than the rest of the electorate – a finding that dates back more than fifty years.

What is less clear is why. What *causes* this? For some (especially some of those on the right), it's all because universities are Marxist Madrasas, full of leftie lecturers proselytising in the classroom when they should be teaching advanced algebra or crop rotation in the fourteenth century.

As someone who has spent all his working life in and around universities, I am aware of this complaint but have always been a bit sceptical about the idea that academics have much direct impact on their students' views. Given that they pay so little attention when I'm talking to them about departmental select committees or Early Day Motions, it has always seemed unlikely that I'd manage to shift their fundamental values all that much, even if I wanted to. I'd be happy enough if I got them to look at the reading list occasionally.

But if it's not their time in the classroom, then what causes graduates to have different values? Alternative explanations focus on a process of selection – that is, graduates are more liberal because liberals are more likely to go to university – or post-graduation sorting – graduates are more liberal because after university they earn on average more money and work in more liberal occupations, where they hang out with more liberal people.

Disentangling these effects is incredibly difficult, because it requires data on attitudes over time or on people's pre-university views and values. But two recent research papers, published within weeks of one another, attempted to work their way through this Gordian knot and came to broadly similar conclusions: a university education does have a direct impact on someone's political attitudes, but it is much less than you might think – and not always in the obvious direction.

For example, Ralph Scott, one of the authors of the papers, utilised the 1970 Cohort Study, which enabled him to track the attitudes of individuals throughout their life and revealed some evidence of a direct university effect. Going to university lowered levels of racial prejudice by a small amount, as well as making respondents less authoritarian. You might note that, being a study of the 1970 cohort, this is data on mostly people now in their fifties and who graduated over thirty years ago, and you might, to misquote L. P. Hartley, believe that university then was a foreign country, where they did things differently.

But another paper by Elizabeth Simon, using more recent data from between 1994 and 2020, finds something similar. Using household data, which allowed her to examine siblings, comparing those who go to university with those who don't, she found that the apparent effect of a university education reduces by around 70 per cent once you control for family background. In other words, what looks like the effect of going to university is almost all explained by the type of people who choose to go.

There is still an effect, though. Going to university does result, for example, in you having more liberal attitudes to gender roles. But once you control for pre-university selection, the size of these effects is fairly small. How small? Put crudely, on a 0–100 scale, Scott's largest finding is that university moves someone's views by about seven points, Simon's by at most one point. These are the largest findings and the latter is almost homeopathic levels of influence.

The kicker is that both these papers – using different time periods and different methods – also find that university does not always liberalise. Simon found that the direct effect of a university education was to make people *less* environmentally friendly, and both pieces of research found that when it came to attitudes towards the economy, university made people more *right*-wing. Again, the differences are small to vanishing, but they are not quite what you'd expect from a Marxist Madrasa. If my more left-wing colleagues really are proselytising, then they are not very good at it.

That'll be 9,000 quid a year, please.

Further reading

R. Scott, 'Does university make you more liberal? Estimating the within-individual effects of higher education on political values', *Electoral Studies* (2022).

E. Simon, 'Demystifying the link between higher education and liberal values: A within-sibship analysis of British individuals' attitudes from 1994–2020', *British Journal of Sociology* (2022).

M. Sobolewska and R. Ford, *Brexitland* (2020).

CHAPTER 8

FIGHTS

In 1951, the MP for Knutsford is said to have kicked the Belgian ambassador down a flight of stairs. A former soldier and boxer, Colonel Walter Bromley-Davenport MP was a whip of the old-school variety; thinking he had spotted one of his flock daring to leave Westminster before the 10 p.m. vote without authorisation, he dispensed summary justice. This case of mistaken identity was enough to end Bromley-Davenport's tenure in the Conservative Whips' Office, where he was replaced by a young Edward Heath.

That's how the story is usually told, anyway – although in Heath's version, it was an MP who got kicked and the ambassador was apocryphal. Either way, I have always thought it revealing about the way whipping was then conducted that most versions of this story imply that had it been an MP, it would have been just fine and dandy.

And whatever happened, it was an unusual but not unique

incident. Eugene Wolfe's *Dangerous Seats* contains multiple examples of physical violence at Westminster. These peaked in the seventeenth and eighteenth centuries, but as late as 1914, one MP was offering another 'satisfaction in any form of combat he desired' and there are dozens of more recent examples of fisticuffs or similar.

A recently published piece of research studied parliamentary brawls across almost forty years in more than 200 countries. The resulting database goes by the title 'Fistfights In parliamentary Sessions Time-Series' (FISTS for short) and contains 375 separate acts of violence, close to four times the number of cases than were previously known about.

Even this figure almost certainly underestimates their actual frequency. Older cases are harder to detect using online searches and not all brawls become public – or at least that's what I've been told.

It is also not always easy to decide what counts as an act of violence. Fights in the chamber, obviously. But how would we code Bromley-Davenport, who may or may not have assaulted another MP but at least thought he was doing so? What about heavy-handed whipping? Do we count the events in October 2022 during a vote on fracking, when there were accusations that MPs were 'physically manhandled' into the division lobbies?

Or what about drunken altercations in Strangers' Bar, as in 2012, when the Labour MP Eric Joyce headbutted one Tory

MP and punched one of his own whips? That particular fight is sometimes said to have been especially consequential. The theory goes something like this: Joyce was charged and said he would resign his seat; the selection of his replacement in Falkirk became embroiled in accusations of rigging; that then led to Ed Miliband changing the rules for Labour membership, including allowing people to pay just a few pounds to get involved in leadership elections, a rule change that proved a boost to Jeremy Corbyn's campaign to become leader; Corbyn's lacklustre campaigning during the Brexit referendum helped depress the Labour vote and lead to Britain leaving the EU. It's a theory, anyway. Joyce himself was of the view that if it 'hadn't been Falkirk it would have been somewhere else', which is probably correct – and it's not too difficult to spot other flaws in the argument.

In this case, the researchers went for a narrow definition, focusing on acts by MPs in Parliament that were about parliamentary business. So, Eric Joyce doesn't count – we can also exclude his arrest a year later after another fight – and we can treat 375 as a minimum figure.

We could still note that these instances remain relatively infrequent. In over two-thirds of the countries studied, there were zero such cases. Even in the countries where they did occur, they average about one a decade. Brawling in Parliament is a breach of democratic norms, but when extremely contentious matters are being discussed, tempers can run high. We might expect things to boil over occasionally.

Perhaps more interesting, though, is *where* they take place. There is no evidence that having more women in a parliament reduces the propensity of its members to fight. (Who remembers Bernadette Devlin slapping the Home Secretary in 1972?) MPs fight more in parliaments when the majority is slim or where there are lots of smaller parties. You also don't tend to get many fights in parliaments in authoritarian regimes (what's the point?) or in places with high levels of electoral democracy. The problems mostly come with those in between – countries where the legislatures are important enough to matter but where democracy is not functioning quite well enough.

Although for the most part it is better to be a lover than a fighter, one intriguing interpretation of this research is that parliamentary violence isn't always negative. It can be a sign that a parliament is beginning to matter more, as previously autocratic states become more open; hence why the Russian Duma started to see punch-ups in the 1990s. On the other hand, if we start to see fights in states that were previously settled democracies, it could be a sign of democratic backsliding.

It is perhaps not setting the bar very high, but for all the pressures that British politics have come under in recent years, at least MPs haven't started punching each other in the Chamber. It is one behavioural norm that seems to have survived. If they start, we should be worried.

Further reading

M. Schmoll and W. L. Ting, 'Explaining Physical Violence in Parliaments', *Journal of Conflict Resolution* (2023).

E. Wolfe, *Dangerous Seats: Parliamentary Violence in the United Kingdom* (2019).

CHAPTER 9

PREFERENCES

Fellow lecturer to me, after a *Question Time*-style event: 'What did you think of that?'

Me: 'It was alright, but didn't that dreadful woman remind you why you don't vote Lib Dem?'

Him: 'That's my wife.'

It may have been years ago, but the embarrassment still lingers. It came flooding back to me recently while reading some of the excellent new research that is starting to be published on the 2024 general election.

Psephologists and commentators often focus on which parties voters like and want to vote for. Yet the more you read about the 2024 contest, the more it becomes clear that as the party system fragments – and the combined vote share for Labour and the Conservatives last year was the lowest since Labour emerged as a significant party in 1918 – we also need to focus much more on who voters *don't* like and who they *won't* vote for.

Take, for example, the extent to which supporters of different parties voted depending on what they perceived as the tactical situation in their constituency. As a fascinating new piece of research, recently published in *Political Quarterly*, makes clear, Labour, Liberal Democrat and Green supporters voted in very different ways, depending on what was going on locally – and with the aim of causing maximum hurt to the Conservatives.

In constituencies in which they believed the top two parties to be Labour and the Conservatives, those voters who preferred Labour were almost certain to indeed vote Labour, but of those who would have preferred the Liberal Democrats, under half voted for their actual preferred party. In seats where it was the Liberal Democrats who were duking it out with the Tories, the proportions were almost exactly reversed: those who liked the Lib Dems voted Lib Dem, but just over half of those who would have preferred Labour stuck with their preferred party.

The voting system used at Westminster may not allow voters to register a second preference, but they do still have them. For Labour, the Lib Dems and the Greens, between 73 and 80 per cent of their voters back another party of the left as their second choice. For Reform voters, their second preference was overwhelmingly the Conservatives (72 per cent). But Conservatives did not reciprocate as strongly. About half had Reform as their second-placed party, but the remainder was spread between other parties. What percentage of Conservative voters said their second preference was either Lib Dem or Green? You win a coconut if you said 37 per cent.

But the real kicker is that whereas many supporters of left-wing parties responded to the tactical situation in their constituency, voters on the right mostly did not. In seats where Labour and the Conservatives were fighting, most of those who preferred Reform voted Reform. Where it was Reform fighting Labour, most Conservatives voted Conservative. As the authors write: 'Reform voters were no more likely to vote Conservative if they thought Labour could win a constituency or if they thought the Liberal Democrats would win a constituency.'

The research is good on why these effects were not even more significant. For one thing, while many voters will vote tactically, most still do not. Plus, many misperceive the tactical situation in their seat. People were much less likely to think they were in Labour versus Conservative contests than they actually were – and much more likely to think they were in Labour versus Lib Dem fights than in reality.

This is one of the reasons why Labour could move from catastrophic defeat to glorious landslide within five years, despite an increase in vote share of just 1 percentage point. In the majority of seats that Labour already held – albeit, given the boundary changes, nominally – its vote share went down. But it went up in most of the seats Labour needed to win. That 1 percentage point figure was an average; there were very few constituencies where Labour's vote share went up by just 1 point.

The result was an extremely efficiently distributed vote. In 2019, just over half the votes cast for the Labour Party were wasted (in the psephological sense) in that they went to candidates who lost. In 2024, the equivalent figure was just 22 per cent. The percentage of effective votes – those required to elect a Labour candidate – went up by around 10 percentage points.

The problem with your vote being efficiently distributed, however, is that it can then become inefficient very quickly. It's possible to see multiple ways in which these factors could play out differently next time. What if, now that one of the parties is in government, voters on the left stop obliging? What if voters on the right start to?

I have slight qualms about the question asked to determine preferences, which is whether you 'like' the party concerned. We all have a friend who we like very much but who we would not trust to look after our house or our kids. But still, one stat buried in the appendices should worry the Conservatives. When voters were asked which party they most liked, the Conservatives were not in the top two. Indeed, they were not even in the top three. Labour topped the poll and Reform and the Greens came second and third respectively, with the Lib Dems fifth. The Conservatives were fourth.

Further reading

M. Miori and J. Green, 'The Most Disproportionate UK Election: How the Labour Party Doubled its Seat Share with a 1.6-Point Increase in Vote Share in 2024', *Political Quarterly* (2025).

CHAPTER 10

NEWBIES

The day before my wedding, en route with my wife-to-be to a rehearsal and running well behind schedule, I stopped to take a photo of a street sign. 'I say, darling, would you mind telling me what you are doing?' she asked. At least it was something like that – I may not have got the precise words right. 'It's Milk Street,' I replied. 'It played an important part in the 1975 Tory leadership contest.' 'Oh, for fuck's sake,' she said. I have definitely remembered that last bit correctly.

Six individuals stood as candidates in that contest, from which Margaret Thatcher emerged victorious. Only one of them, Sir Geoffrey Howe, had been in the House of Commons for less than ten years. Indeed, of the fifty-three candidates for the leadership of the three main British political parties in the sixteen leadership contests between 1963 and 1994, only five had under a decade's experience in the Commons at the point at which they stood. Howe aside, the other four were Liberals or Liberal

Democrats. Collectively, these five constituted fewer than 10 per cent of all the candidates. The newbies were the outliers.

Compare that with now. The winner of the 2024 Conservative leadership contest, Kemi Badenoch, had been an MP for just seven years when she became party leader and yet that was her second leadership contest. The runner-up, Robert Jenrick, had been in the Commons for ten years. James Cleverly and Tom Tugendhat, who came third and fourth respectively, had both been MPs for under a decade. The *most* experienced candidates, Mel Stride and Priti Patel, had fourteen years' Commons experience each – but they were the first two eliminated.

Nor are these the exceptions. Of the eight candidates who fought the first Conservative leadership contest in 2022, won by Liz Truss, only Jeremy Hunt had had more than twelve years in the Commons under his belt – and he went out in the first round. When Rishi Sunak replaced Truss later the same year, he had been an MP for seven years, taken part in two leadership contests and become Prime Minister. Of all of Britain's premiers, only Pitt the Younger, who reached the top after just three years, had less experience in Parliament.

It's not just a Conservative thing. Of the three candidates who contested Labour's leadership in 2020, the most experienced, Lisa Nandy, had only been an MP for a decade; both the first- and second-placed candidates had been MPs for a mere five years.

When John Major entered Downing Street in 1990, the average

length of parliamentary experience for Prime Ministers before taking office was almost twenty-six years. (I owe this fact to *Facts About the British Prime Ministers*, a book so invaluable that I own three copies, so as never to be without.) Having been in the Commons for less than twelve years, Major was then a real outlier. Since him, however, we've had Sunak (seven), Cameron (nine), Starmer (nine), Johnson (eleven, albeit not continuously), Truss (twelve) and Blair (fourteen). Only May and Brown bucked this trend, but neither for very long, and even both of their parliamentary tenures were still below the pre-Major average.

I first made this point over a decade ago, when the three major parties were all led by people – David Cameron, Ed Miliband and Nick Clegg – who assumed the leadership having served at most a term in the House of Commons. In the case of Clegg, it was just two years. Indeed, at the time they became the leaders of their parties, Cameron and Miliband were not just the least experienced leaders of their parties in the post-war era but the least experienced *candidates*.

The contrast with what came before was stark. Prior to Miliband, the average post-war Labour leader had nineteen years of parliamentary experience under their belt. Prior to Cameron, the average Conservative had twenty-two. There are obviously still some exceptions to the rise of the newbie – Jeremy Corbyn and Theresa May had reasonable parliamentary experience, as did Ed Davey. But it is now the old hands who are the outliers. Something has changed.

It is partly the consequence of a speeding up of parliamentary careers, with MPs spending less time in the Commons. In 2019, almost a third (32 per cent) of those retiring from the Commons had less than a decade's experience, while around a quarter (23 per cent) had done twenty-five years or more on the green benches. But in 1970, the equivalent figures were 12 per cent and 46 per cent. In other words, in 1970, the number of long-serving retirees was almost four times greater than those jumping ship early; in 2019 the latter outnumbered the former. The House of Commons elected in 2024 was spectacularly inexperienced. A full 80 per cent were first elected in 2017 or after – so had just seven years' experience – and more than half came in at the 2024 election itself.

It's also about the growing importance of significant pre-parliamentary political experience among some senior politicians. Ed Miliband and David Cameron had both been special advisers, for example, before becoming MPs. Nick Clegg had been an MEP; Kemi Badenoch and James Cleverly had been members of the London Assembly. Boris Johnson was Mayor of London before his second term as an MP.

But whatever the cause, this change has consequences for Parliament itself. Historically, one of its key functions was as a recruitment pool and training ground for would-be ministers and party leaders. It still retains its near-monopoly status on ministerial ambition – the only way to the top remains through the Commons – but its value as a place where would-be leaders are tested and tried out appears to be on the wane. There is a lot of talk, often misguided and historically inaccurate, about parliamentary decline; yet here is one place where the role of the Commons does appear to be changing.

We currently have a very inexperienced government being scrutinised by a very inexperienced House of Commons. Maybe that is why things are going so well?

Further reading

S. Barber, 'Arise, Careerless Politician: The Rise of the Professional Party Leader', *Politics* (2014).

P. Cowley, 'Arise, Novice Leader! The Continuing Rise of the Career Politician in Britain', *Politics* (2012).

CHAPTER 11

PROJECTION

It's the political science equivalent of shooting fish in a barrel. You poll the public with factual questions about politics or the economy. The results demonstrate an imperfect relationship between beliefs and reality. Hey presto – an article. 'British public wrong about nearly everything,' as a headline in *The Independent* once put it, when the public thought 31 per cent of the population were immigrants and £24 out of every £100 spent on benefits was claimed fraudulently. The official figures were 13 per cent and £0.70.

I'm not knocking it. Done well, this sort of work can be a useful corrective, reminding us of how voters perceive the world. Bobby Duffy's book *The Perils of Perception* is packed full of examples that show the problem is not just confined to Brits either. What percentage of Brazilian girls aged fifteen to nineteen give birth each year? 6.7 per cent. What was the average guess by Brazilians? 48 per cent.

When there were just four Muslim MPs, a survey I did found that the average response from the British voter was that some 14 per cent of the Commons was Muslim – that would have been ninety MPs. There were at the time thirteen MPs who publicly identified as gay and lesbian; the public thought there were 116.

Yet it turns out that misperceptions of reality are not confined to voters. Two fascinating pieces of recently published research show that politicians can get things badly wrong too.

One article, in the *British Journal of Political Science*, reported US politicians' knowledge about levels of economic hardship. Not so much a 'price of milk' question – more a series of 'how many of my voters can afford milk' questions. Testing knowledge about financial insecurity, affordable healthcare and university debt, a survey of 1,265 candidates running for election in state legislatures found that most answers were seriously wrong – although somewhat to the evident surprise of the researcher, the politicos had a tendency to *over*estimate the levels of hardship in their areas.

Lurking in this sort of research is often the assumption that people would hold different views if they had the correct information ('if only they knew'). One nice feature of this piece of work was that it presented a sample of respondents with the correct answers, before asking them some related policy questions, while other politicians were asked the same questions but without the correct information. Your assumption might be that these two groups would give different responses. They didn't.

Knowledge of the actual data made no difference to their views at all.

Another recent piece of research, out in *Political Psychology*, looked at politicians' perceptions of the attitudes of their constituents. They polled voters in four countries – Belgium, Canada, Germany and Switzerland – about a range of policies (for example, 'Canada should increase the number of immigrants it admits each year'), while simultaneously asking politicians what they *thought* voters would say.

They found clear evidence of projection – that is, assuming that others share your own beliefs. For example, politicians who 'totally agreed' with a policy estimated public agreement on that issue to be on average 24 percentage points higher than politicians who totally disagreed with it. Projection was especially strong when it came to their own supporters, rather than the general public.

Both of these papers also ran the same tests with voters and found that in three out of the four countries surveyed, they were no less accurate than their political masters. Sure, they too got things wrong and engaged in industrial-level projection, but they were no worse offenders than politicians. 'Politicians also wrong about nearly everything,' you might say.

This isn't always a problem. Sometimes politicians project their views onto the public, only for the public and politicians to be in agreement anyway. Plus, not all political decisions are driven by concerns about public opinion; if you've decided on a policy regardless, you might care less what the public think. Still, in those cases where the public and politicians do differ, it can matter – not least because it means politicians underestimate the extent to which the public disagree with them. Maybe you have decided to do something regardless of public opinion – but it would still help to know whether you were doing it with the support of the public or despite their opposition. And since the effect was largest when it came to politicians' own supporters – the people they really do want to keep onside – the potential problems with projection are, as the authors remark, 'largest where they are likely most consequential'.

The observant reader will have noticed that the UK was not one of the countries studied. Perhaps British politicians would not suffer from these flaws. Maybe they would, instead, have a deep understanding of the issues facing their constituents and be entirely in touch with the views of their voters. Or maybe not.

A postscript: since I first wrote the original column, a more recent paper, which reanalysed the data from the same four countries, found that politicians were more accurate at estimating public opinion when politicians thought an issue was more salient – that is, when it mattered more – to voters (and also when an issue was important to them personally). But there was no clear and consistent relationship between politicians' perceptual accuracy and actual public salience. In other words, politicians' perceptions of the views of the public were more accurate when politicians perceived that they cared, but their perceptions of whether the public cared owed little to reality...

Further reading

C. Butler et al., 'Politicians are better at estimating public opinion when they think it is more salient', *Party Politics* (2024).

J. Sevenans et al., 'Projection in Politicians' Perceptions of Public Opinion', *Political Psychology* (2023).

A. Thal, 'Do Political Elites Have Accurate Perceptions of Social Conditions?', *British Journal of Political Science* (2023).

CHAPTER 12

LAWNS

How does your garden grow? One of the earliest conversations I ever had with an MP was about how, when canvassing, he claimed to be able to predict which party someone would support based on the state of their lawn. At the time I thought this seemed unlikely, bordering on delusional, but in the decades since, I've had multiple chats with MPs and activists along similar lines. In John O'Farrell's book about his time in the Labour Party, *Things Can Only Get Better*, he grudgingly admits that Conservatives take greater care over the appearance of their homes than do those on the left; their cars are cleaner, he says, their windowsills neater. Long before he became a political columnist at the *FT*, a young Stephen Bush used to play a game to see if he could predict the voting intention of the people he was canvassing based only on their front doors and windows. A messy window box was a giveaway, apparently.

It's not inherently implausible. It might be a noisy cue, with lots of exceptions, and maybe one that would vary geographically, but there is plenty of research that shows opposing political tribes demonstrate differences in other non-political aspects of their lives: American conservatives have tidier bedrooms, for example, compared to American liberals. I tried once to do something similar with food. Even controlling for age, class and education, we found the more right-wing the party that people supported, the more likely they were to favour prawns, bacon, steak and kidney pie, smoked salmon and avocado – and to dislike tofu. If it holds for bedrooms and cuisine, maybe it holds for horticulture and house decor?

A fascinating research paper published recently attempted to test something similar, albeit based on more conventional cues. If you knew someone's class, age and education, how likely would you be to be able to predict their vote? The researchers tested this by showing respondents profiles of voters and then asking them to say how they thought that person had voted – either in the 2017 election or in the Brexit referendum the year before.

You try it. Imagine a 27-year-old white man with no religious affiliation. He is a graduate owner-occupier living in the East Midlands earning somewhere between £60,000 and £99,999. He considers himself working class, as he did while growing up. How did he vote in 2017?

A neat aspect of this paper is that each of the profiles that respondents were shown were of real voters – people who had previously taken part in the British Election Study. As a result, we know exactly how they had behaved at the ballot box and could compare respondents' guesses with the reality. (In case you were wondering, that 27-year-old voted Conservative.)

The paper concluded that, on average, respondents had a pretty good understanding of the factors that underpinned people's votes. They were more likely to predict a high probability of a Leave vote when the individual really was a Leave voter and ditto for Conservatives. Plus, respondents who were more interested in politics were more likely to get it right. These differences were not all that substantial – plenty of people got things wrong – but they were statistically significant.

There was, however, a lag in how respondents saw the world. People tended to overemphasise class differences – which are now less significant than they used to be – but underestimate more recent electoral cleavages, such as age and education. Indeed, education was the only variable where people got the direction wrong, thinking voters with degrees were more likely to be Conservative than Labour, when the opposite is now true.

One other aspect of the work really struck me. Respondents were asked to say how sure they were about their estimates – and they often went for extremes, saying that there was 0 per cent or 100 per cent probability that someone had voted in a certain way, even though a moment's thought would indicate that such levels of certainty were unwise.

In part, this sort of finding just reflects how people struggle with probabilities – but it also, I think, reflects the fact that we often talk about demographic characteristics as somehow determining someone's vote when they do not. They are almost always probabilistic, rather than deterministic. Conservative supporters are *more likely* to like bacon and are *less likely* to like tofu; it is not that all Conservative supporters like bacon and none of them eats tofu. The same, no doubt, would be true of messy window boxes or tidy lawns.

But think of how we talked about the Brexit referendum: the middle class voted Remain, as did the young and minority ethnic voters and graduates; the working class, the old and those who did not go to university voted Leave.

True, the majority of voters in each of these groups did indeed back that outcome, but there were millions, literally millions, of exceptions who too often got written out of the narrative. There are a whole series of overlooked Brexit tribes – old Remainers, graduate Leavers, minority ethnic Leavers, working-class Remainers, middle-class Leavers – who still get almost completely ignored in most discussion of 2016.

For understandable methodological reasons, the research paper only tested binaries – Remain/Leave or Labour/Conservative. Yet even in the referendum there was a third option – to not vote. Often, once you factor in non-voters you find things are even more complicated. In Scotland, for example, while more people voted Remain than Leave, once you take into account non-voters, a random Scot is more likely not to have voted Remain than to have done so. Other elections have long since ceased to offer binary choices, all of which makes predicting someone's vote – based on their background or their lawn – even harder than it used to be.

Further reading

D. R. Carney et al., 'The Secret Lives of Liberals and Conservatives: Personality Profiles, Interaction Styles, and the Things They Leave Behind', *Political Psychology* (2008).

N. Titelman and B. Lauderdale, 'Can citizens guess how other citizens voted based on demographic characteristics?', *Political Science Research and Methods* (2023).

CHAPTER 13

WINNERS

I n his 1936 book, the American political scientist Harold Lasswell famously defined politics as who gets what, when and how. Various pieces of research from the US have shown that the answer to the first part of Lasswell's question is that policies supported by the rich get implemented more often than those supported by the poor. Some fascinating research recently published in the *British Journal of Political Science* has revealed that the same sort of policy congruence applies across Europe.

The researchers found that policies supported by the richest people in Europe (by which they mean those in the top 20 per cent of income) get implemented more often than those supported by the poorest (the bottom 20 per cent). The success rate of the middle 60 per cent of incomes sits – as you might expect – somewhere in the middle.

This is one of those bits of research that is a lot easier said than done. For one thing, you need to find testable survey questions

– that is, ones that have asked about things that could be implemented (or not). A lot of opinion polling is much more general, asking about priorities, preferences or attitudes. This research required specific policies. Should the law be X? Should we spend more on Y?

You also need to be able to break the polling findings down by income. And then you need to go and check whether each policy was implemented or not. Is the law now X? Do we now spend more on Y? To have tested this, as this paper does, with some 3,000 policy proposals is therefore an impressive feat of research.

Yet for all that you might be impressed by the work involved, you might well think the conclusion isn't especially revelatory. The rich getting their own way? The poor not? To channel Claude Rains in *Casablanca*: 'I'm shocked. Shocked!'

Stick with it, though. For one thing, even if you've long suspected something, it's always nice to have it confirmed. But there are, I think, other things about this work that make it more interesting than the headline.

The first is the scale of the difference between the richest and the poorest. It was about 3 percentage points. That is, enacted policies were supported (on average) by 3 per cent more of the richest than the poorest citizens. You might be surprised – I know I was – at how *small* this difference is. It is, in the words of the paper's title, a slight edge.

One reason for this – and it's an interesting finding in itself – is that the views of the richest and the poorest often aren't all that different. This correlation is a common finding from the US studies into this topic, and it is one of the reasons why even though there clearly is an effect, it is not as great as you might expect.

Also striking is how consistent it is. The researchers found the same effect across most issues they examined, across time and across countries. The study spans thirty-eight years, with the rich getting their way a majority of the time in thirty-four of them. The rich got their way in two-thirds of issues studied and the poor did better than the rich in just two out of the twenty-one European countries studied. The UK wasn't one of the two.

And while a 3 per cent difference may not sound like much, over time it is significant. Although it's not a perfect comparison, a European roulette table, for example, has a house advantage of just under 3 per cent. That's a slight edge. Maybe roulette's not your thing, so let's try blackjack. If you follow basic strategy (and don't count cards), the house has a mere 0.5 per cent edge. That's even slighter. You can certainly play and win big at both blackjack and roulette. But over time, if you play enough, there is only one outcome. The same seems to be true in politics.

And the third interesting point is that while the effect was consistent in almost every country, the scale of the effect wasn't. The rich got their way more in some European countries than others, and the differences between countries were larger than the differences between the rich and the poor within countries. The within-country differences ranged, in most cases, between 2 and 5 per cent. It's never massive, but it's almost always there.

To explain these inter-country differences, the researchers examined things like economic inequality, campaign finance regulation (or the lack thereof), levels of union membership and voter turnout. We might perhaps expect that the poor's views would be more marginalised in countries with greater income inequality. Or, strongly inspired by the US experience, perhaps we would get greater differences in countries where campaign finance laws allow the rich more influence and where he who pays the piper calls the tune?

Or maybe countries with stronger trade unions would see smaller differences, with unions better able to keep left-of-centre issues on the agenda, regardless of the party in power? Or would we find that it's all to do with who votes and these differences would be greater in those countries where the poor vote less than the rich – on the principle that if you ain't voting, they ain't listening.

And yet, while all these theories sound plausible, it turns out that none of them made the slightest difference. When the paper analysed them, they got a series of null effects. For ye have the poor always with you but not their policy preferences, as it doesn't quite say in Matthew 26:11.

Further reading

M. Persson and A. Sundell, 'The Rich Have a Slight Edge: Evidence from Comparative Data on Income-Based Inequality in Policy Congruence', *British Journal of Political Science* (2023).

CHAPTER 14

POTHOLES

The school run takes less than ten minutes. In that time, we pass at least four potholes with the potential to take out a tyre; one is so deep, it must be halfway to Australia. In the dark, with other drivers swerving wildly as they spot them at the last minute, the journey is suitable only for a hardened thrill-seeker. Data published by the Department of Transport shows that the roads of rural East Sussex are far from the worst in the country, so this experience may be a familiar one to many readers.

Were it not for the need to focus with a laser-like intensity on the road ahead, my mind would drift to some research, published a few years ago, on the politics of potholes. Based on elections in San Diego, it found a link between the state of the roads in parts of the city and electoral support for the incumbent politician.

Holes in the road don't immediately sound like the stuff of high politics; there isn't a *West Wing* episode about them. But they do matter. Their direct importance to drivers – and especially cyclists and motorcyclists, for whom they are even more dangerous – is obvious. But it's more the frequency with which we encounter them. We might go for weeks, months or even years without interacting with other bits of the state, but roads are something that many people encounter daily. A UK survey in 2024 found that potholes were among the top five things voters said they wanted to see political parties talk about in their campaigning materials. And more generally, if the roads are crumbling, it is hard not to see it as a metaphor for the wider state of the nation's infrastructure.

San Diego was a good city to choose for the study because the roads there had not – contra Ron Burgundy – stayed classy. Voters had noticed that the US's self-proclaimed finest city had some of the country's worst roads (ironic for a city that also has the nickname 'City in Motion') and the issue ranked highly among the things they cared about. In one survey, the condition of the city streets emerged as voters' number-one concern.

The researchers got hold of a database of 52,000 complaints about the city's roads. They found that places with more potholes were less likely to vote for the incumbent, even once you controlled for previous levels of electoral support. The effect held for two different types of political offices and across multiple political cycles. Each pothole complaint had the effect of lowering an incumbent's vote share by 0.2 percentage points; applied where

I live, an effect of this size would likely result in some politicians polling less than zero.

The main reason for liking the article is not just that you must respect any research where one of the independent variables is 'Pothole Complaints' but also that it is a good example of what political scientists call retrospective voting. That is, elections can be a judgement on the record of incumbents, rather than being prospective about what politicians say they will do. There's lots of evidence from the UK and elsewhere that retrospective voting is tremendously important and far more so than a lot of the media coverage of elections implies.

It's perfectly understandable. For voters who don't pay much attention to politics – that is, most of them – retrospective voting has the advantage that it is low-cost. It does not require voters to analyse promises and pledges made by the parties. People just need to focus on what life has been like over the past few years. Are the roads dangerous? Are they getting better or worse? These are much easier questions to answer than worrying about the minutiae of a party's manifesto. If they are getting better, then you can reward the incumbent. If not, you can punish them. In addition, while anyone can promise you something ('I will improve your roads'), their record is much harder to dodge ('But you didn't'). Even the most disconnected of voters will notice when things are going very obviously wrong.

In reality, the causal relationships are often much more

complicated. Maybe you're better off (or not) because the global economy has picked up (or not), rather than because of anything the government has done. Maybe the schools are better (or worse) now because of decisions made years before the current government came into power. But then politicians are happy to take the credit for things beyond their control, so they can't really complain when they get the downside.

This is another reason why the potholes paper is so neat. In San Diego, responsibility for the state of the roads was entirely the city's. Voters had a pretty good idea of who to blame – although even in San Diego, most of the *causes* of the problems with the roads predated the incumbent politicians.

The lines of accountability for roads in the UK are much less clear. Different bodies maintain different roads. Even if it's a local authority-maintained road, they operate under a funding regime where they are not entirely free to raise and spend at will. The announcement in 2025 by the Labour government of significant investment for pothole repairs illustrates this problem. Local councils will be repairing roads with money provided by the central government; if the roads get better, do I thank the council or the government? If they don't get better, who do I blame?

This is, I suspect, why similar attempts in the UK to test whether poorly performing councils get punished at the polls often fail to determine any similar effect. It may also be why my suspension needs fixing.

Further reading

C. Burnett and V. Kogan, 'The Politics of Potholes: Service Quality and Retrospective Voting in Local Elections', *Journal of Politics* (2017).

CHAPTER 15

OBVIOUSLY

What if I were to tell you about recently published research which demonstrated that voters judged female politicians negatively compared to their male counterparts? I suspect some of you would mentally file it away under Statements of the Bleeding Obvious: 'I can't believe academics waste their time studying this sort of stuff', 'Tell me something I don't know', 'Well, duh, obviously' and so on.

Which is why you should want to read about some recent research that showed you'd be wrong.

Let's start with a fascinating study just out in the journal *Political Behavior*, which reveals that British voters essentially judge male and female politicians the same.

These sorts of biases are not straightforward to test. Straight up ask people their views ('Are you sexist?') and people give what they think are socially correct answers. Ask people about actual politicians ('What do you think of Liz Truss?') and you have to disentangle all sorts of other things – do they like or dislike them because of their party, their policies or whatever (and do they even know them?).

You can try to test it by looking at actual election results – do male candidates outperform female ones? – but again, you need to disentangle all sorts of other factors that might be driving what's going on, including whether the candidates are of equal quality. If, say, the female candidates were on average not as good as the male ones (as a result of positive discrimination or similar), then their doing less well could be evidence of quality control, not sexism. Conversely, however, if the female candidates were of better quality on average than the male ones (because they have had to fight harder to be selected in the first place, for which there is plenty of evidence), then even if they polled just as well at the ballot box, this might still be evidence of sexism. In other words, the results can only get you so far – although, for the record, evidence of direct electoral penalties based on gender are now very slim indeed, at least in the UK.

So, a good way to get at this is with profiles of hypothetical politicians. At its simplest, you ask half a bunch of survey respondents to give their views on a 46-year-old former accountant called David and the other half to judge a 46-year-old former accountant called Sarah. In the absence of any gender bias, the two sub-samples should respond more or less the same. But if they don't? Ta-da!

One of the many benefits of this type of work is that respondents don't know what it is that you are trying to test when they complete their surveys, which makes it harder for them to give the socially correct response. More sophisticated versions of this approach use a technique called conjoint analysis, which allows you to vary multiple characteristics in the profiles and then isolate the effect of each change.

When the researchers did this with profiles of imaginary politicians in Britain, they found some clear results. Voters responded to the amount of work that the politician was said to have done; they liked MPs who worked hard and this was especially true for those who focused on constituency stuff, which was valued more than Chamber or committee work. This can be added to a long line of research papers showing how much voters value the work MPs do in their constituencies, variously mentioned in the chapters that follow.

The more interesting finding, though, was that there was almost no effect when the researchers changed the sex of the MPs. If anything, on some things that were being tested, the hypothetical female MPs were slightly more favoured, albeit by a small margin. As the authors write, they found 'no evidence of gender bias in voter evaluations of politicians' productivity in office. There is no significant difference in voter evaluations of high- or low-performing MPs' job performance, electability, or preferences for men and women, and voters harbour no outright preference for men over women.'

This chimes with another paper published recently, which drew on sixty-seven separate studies into the sort of politicians that people preferred. Many of these studies were not designed to study gender specifically, but they all included it as one of the characteristics they varied. This allowed the researchers to pull the characteristics together and compile a meta-analysis, in which they compared the effect of gender across all the pieces of research.

On average, they found clear evidence of a boost for female politicians of about 1.8 percentage points. These sixty-seven studies came from all over the world, covering six continents. The positive effects were not uniform and didn't exist everywhere; there was, in the words of the authors, 'evidence of heterogeneity across contexts, candidates, and respondents'. But in over three-quarters of the studies, being a woman was an electoral advantage.

Of the ten studies that were included from the UK, nine found women politicians receiving higher ratings than men. As with the first paper, these effects were often small (and not always statistically significant), but what was clear was the absence of any negative effect. When we note the relative absence of female politicians from political institutions, therefore, we know the problem is not the voters.

For all the biases that may exist elsewhere, here's some good news. Maybe it's not so bleeding obvious after all?

Further reading

L. Hargrave and J. C. Smith, 'Working Hard or Hardly Working?

Gender and Voter Evaluations of Legislator Productivity', *Political Behavior* (2023).

S. Schwarz and A. Coppock, 'What Have We Learned about Gender from Candidate Choice Experiments? A Meta-Analysis of Sixty-Seven Factorial Survey Experiments', *Journal of Politics* (2022).

CHAPTER 16

ROLES

In 1955, the *Sunday Dispatch* ran a competition in which it asked its readers what characteristics were required for the perfect MP. Entrants had to select six (in the right order) from a list of twenty potential characteristics. A judging panel of three MPs decided the 'correct' answer. 'Sincerity' was in first place, followed by 'regular attendance at Parliament', 'regular visits to the constituency', 'good health', 'has children' and 'loyal to party'. The competition was won by a Mr Fred Mair, from Hatfield, Hertfordshire. He took home a whopping £5,000, worth well over £100,000 today.

A common characteristic of these sort of newspaper competitions was that the editor's decision was final and no correspondence would be entered into. But if you had been allowed to write in, it might have been to point out that the premise of the competition was flawed – because there is no single correct way to be an MP. It's a position with flexibility. You're an MP, but what *sort* of an MP? (Or, as the ten-year-old son of one of those first elected in 2001 asked him: 'Well, it's very nice, but what do you do?')

Donald Searing's magisterial work on the House of Commons in the 1970s, *Westminster's World*, identified four distinct types of backbenchers: 'policy advocates', 'ministerial aspirants', 'constituency members' and 'Parliament men'. The labels are self-explanatory, even if the phrasing of the last reflects the time of the research. While MPs could channel Walt Whitman and contain multitudes, most had a predominant role that fitted into one of these categories.

It's a great book, albeit about a very different Parliament. The interviews for the study were done at a time when Michael Heseltine and Norman Tebbit were singled out as rising stars. It's dated. Although what was most astonishing about *Westminster's World* is the extent to which it was dated even when it came out. The interviews were conducted in the 1970s; the book wasn't published until the mid-1990s. My director of research wouldn't let me get away with that these days.

Yet for all that it's aged, it's easy enough to identify all four of those archetypes in the MPs in the current House of Commons. What has probably changed are the proportions. All the evidence is that the policy advocates – those who wish to influence public policy – have been growing in number for years. MPs of all parties have become much more activist when it comes to policy, much less content just to be loyal servants of the party.

Similarly, the number of Parliament men or women – already the least common category in Searing's study – has been in long-term decline. These were people for whom just 'being there' was sufficient, like Mr Browborough from Trollope's *Phineas Redux*: 'A model member of Parliament, a man who never spoke, constant in his attendance, who wanted nothing, who had plenty of money, who gave dinners, to whom a seat in Parliament was the be-all and the end-all of life.' Fewer MPs these days are content to just be there.

Perhaps the biggest change, though, is the rise of the constituency role, which has grown dramatically. For all that people talk about MPs being cut off from their constituencies, the opposite is true. Spend any time around Westminster and it is difficult not to be struck by how well MPs know their local patch and just how much effort goes into dealing with the constituency.

By the time Searing carried out his interviews, there were already relatively few MPs who did no constituency work – unlike many of the MPs from the 1940s and 1950s who visited their constituencies a handful of times a year or who filed those letters that did arrive (and there weren't very many) in the wastepaper basket. But still, many had what today would be seen as a relatively light level of engagement with the constituency. While there are still MPs who see their primary role as being a constituency MP – that is, one of Searing's constituency members – no MP can now afford to take the detached attitude to the constituency that was previously commonplace. To a greater or lesser extent, MPs today are all constituency members, in a way that would have been inconceivable to a politician in the 1970s.

A fascinating study from a decade or so ago tested whether the ways MPs went about their job was similar or not to what their voters wanted. The researchers presented a sample of voters with a list of eight things that MPs could be doing – three of which were related to the constituency, five of which were to do with Westminster – and asked them to pick the ones that most mattered.

The public were overwhelmingly constituency-focused: of the eight parts of the job listed, two of them were chosen as the most important by a massive 83 per cent of the public. They were 'taking up and responding to issues and problems raised by constituents' and 'being active in the constituency'.

Of the various Westminster-focused roles, the one the public prioritised the most was 'contributing to the development of legislation' – and that was the priority of just 7 per cent of the public. This might come as no surprise; a desire for MPs who work the parish pump hard is ever-present in surveys.

What was innovative about this study, though, was that it then also asked the same questions to MPs and it found that they prioritised the same things. Those exact same two constituency-facing parts of the job were chosen as the most important by 74 per cent of MPs.

Analysing all of the eight tasks together, there was a slightly greater emphasis on the part of voters towards constituency work than that reported by MPs but not by much. What was most striking about the findings wasn't the differences but the similarities.

Further reading

R. Campbell and J. Lovenduski, 'What Should MPs Do? Public and Parliamentarians' Views Compared', *Parliamentary Affairs* (2015).

D. Searing, *Westminster's World* (1994).

CHAPTER 17

PLEDGES

Each of us has at least one book that has changed the way we see the world – and if you don't, you should.

One of mine is *Do Parties Make a Difference?*, first published in 1980 and which I read as an undergraduate. It was the first time I'd found someone trying to measure what governments and political parties actually did. By doing so, it showed that many of the things I thought about politics were just plain wrong.

Among the book's many findings were two that can initially seem contradictory. First, that, contrary to the old saw about politicians and broken promises, political parties have a good record of implementing their manifestos. The book showed that the Conservative government elected in 1970, for example, implemented 80 per cent of the things it had promised in 'A Better Tomorrow'. Of the remainder, it was ambiguous if the manifesto pledge had been carried out or not in about 10 per cent of cases, no action had been taken in about 8 per cent and a slim 1 per cent of instances where the very opposite of the manifesto had been done.

But second, the book also showed that changes in the party of government at election time have only a limited impact on the direction of public policy. This apparent contradiction is relatively easily explained. For all the fuss over them, manifestos amount to only a small proportion of what governments do: the book found that about 11 per cent of legislation brought forward by governments originated in their manifestos. The rest was responses to unforeseen events – or mostly stuff that just bubbled up from within Whitehall. Most public policy is stuff that governments would be carrying out anyway or that they have inherited from their predecessors.

It's not that elections don't matter but that they make *less* difference than the almost constant focus on the electoral battle would indicate or that parties sometimes pretend. As the book's author, Richard Rose, said elsewhere: 'Policy-makers are heirs before they are choosers.' It takes an awfully long time and a lot of effort to turn the oil tanker.

The past forty or so years have seen an enormous amount of research examining some of these claims in more detail, but the finding about parties delivering on their promises has stood up especially well, both in the UK and elsewhere.

To take one example, a recently published piece of research found 258 separate pledges in the 2017 Conservative manifesto

'Forward, Together'. (In passing, we might note that manifesto titles are, for the most part, not overly imaginative.) Even the short-lived and tumultuous May government, operating as it was without a parliamentary majority, managed to implement almost 70 per cent of the things it had said it would do. Hurrah for them.

Yet those 258 pledges were not of equal value. One was to leave the EU. Another was to require schools to have a single point of contact with mental health services. These are both important issues, but it seems unlikely they are seen by many people as *equally* important.

Most previous studies of manifestos had treated all pledges as if they were equal, when they clearly are not. Yet how to measure importance? A handful of studies had tried to weight the importance of individual manifesto pledges based either on how much media attention they received or just on whether the researcher thought they seemed important. In this more recent case, the researchers tried something different: they asked the public which policies they saw as more central to the party's overall platform. You couldn't do this just by asking every survey respondent about every policy, one after the other. Question fatigue would soon set in. If they didn't die of boredom first, their answers would soon cease to have any validity. So instead, the researchers showed people bundles of policies and asked them to compare them. Do that across enough people and you can rank the importance of each policy separately, without having to ask every respondent about every policy.

And when you do, things look noticeably less rosy. The four most important pledges in the 2017 Conservative manifesto – as judged by the public – were to leave the EU, to reduce annual net immigration to below 100,000, to leave the customs union and to leave the single market. Collectively, those four pledges made up almost 30 per cent of the manifesto's overall weight. Policies related to Brexit made up just 5 per cent of the manifesto if weighted equally; weighted according to their importance, that increased seven-fold. The most central promise ('Leave the EU') alone received 9 per cent of all the weight.

Yet by the end of the 2017 parliament, none of the four most important pledges had been implemented. Of what the public saw as the top ten pledges, only four had been carried out. Weighting things equally, the May government managed to deliver 69 per cent of its manifesto. But weight those pledges by their perceived significance to the public and that dropped to below half or 48 per cent. Maybe not so hurrah.

My suspicion is that things would be even worse in terms of the public perception of whether that government did what it said it would – because in reality, the public won't even be aware of some of the less-significant promises that might have been fulfilled, but they will have noticed the very high-profile ones that weren't. To misquote Gertrude Stein: a policy isn't a policy isn't a policy.

Further reading

J. Mellon et al., 'Which Promises Actually Matter? Election Pledge Centrality and Promissory Representation', *Political Studies* (2021).

R. Rose, *Do Parties Make a Difference?* (1980).

CHAPTER 18

FLATS

Professor David Denver, who died in August 2024, began his book *Elections and Voting Behaviour in Britain* with the words: 'Elections are fun.' Which of us would disagree? Now in its sixth edition and much updated (and renamed), it remains perhaps the single best textbook on British electoral behaviour, one that has helped generations of undergraduates – including, many years ago, this one – get through their studies.

Another of David's claims to fame was that he was involved in what is widely believed to be the first field experiment carried out in British psephology. He and a colleague identified two blocks of flats in a safe Labour ward in Dundee, roughly equidistant from their polling station. With the agreement of the local Labour Party – no one else did any canvassing – he arranged for a full-on campaign to take place in one block but the bare minimum to be done in the other.

Published in the *British Journal of Political Science* in 1971, the study showed the impact of campaigning: turnout was 10 percentage points higher in the block with the full-on campaign compared to the control, with Labour's share of the vote up too. Experiments are now de rigueur in the social sciences, but this was cutting-edge stuff at the time. David was always keen to point out that the flats concerned were then seen as desirable places to live but have long since been demolished.

For politicians, many of whom like nothing more than knocking on a stranger's door, the idea that local campaigning has an electoral pay-off may seem obvious – but at the time, it ran counter to much of the understanding of elections, which had increasingly been seen as national-level events, in which all the important action took place on TV. Grassroots campaigning was seen as a relic, carried out to give activists something to do rather than being of any import. David's work helped change that view. He also helped establish a wider study of constituency-level campaigning in the UK, which has now run for thirty years – and has, more broadly, demonstrated the benefits of grassroots campaigning.

A recent article by that team has just been published in *Political Studies*, examining one of the mechanisms by which local campaigns might have such an impact – namely, helping to establish the viability of candidates and campaigns in the voters' eyes.

The research draws on the British Election Study, which has the great advantage of being a panel study – that is, a survey that questions the same people over time, enabling us to track how their views and attitudes have changed. This allows you, in this case, to measure how likely it is a voter thinks that a candidate might win in a seat before the election gets underway and then again during the campaign, once they've had leaflets stuck through their door or similar – and then to compare the two.

Drawing on data from the general elections of 2015, 2017 and 2019, the research shows that perceptions of electoral viability change during a campaign – but, more crucially, one of the key things that makes them change is campaign activity by the local party. As the authors write: 'The more campaign contacts from a particular party a voter received, the greater the improvement in their perceptions of the possibility of that party winning in the constituency.'

Of the nine cases tested (three parties, across three elections), the effect was found in eight – and even in the one case where it doesn't quite achieve statistical significance, the effect was still in the right direction.

It may not surprise you that the effect size varies – or that the largest effect found was with the Lib Dems. (Those 'Lib Dems Winning Here' signs really do work.) Comparing the lowest levels of campaign exposure with the greatest, the improvement in the perception of a candidate's election performance was between 9 and 13 percentage points for Lib Dem candidates. For Labour, the effect was between 4 and 11 points. For the Tories, for the two contests that achieved statistical significance, they were 5 and 6 points.

These aren't large enough effects to persuade voters that a no-hoper candidate is about to romp home, but they could matter in more marginal races. Increased campaign viability could matter in multiple ways – encouraging people to volunteer or enabling tactical voting. Or in some cases, it might allow voters to vote for the person they most want to win but previously thought was out of the race.

Some caveats: measuring local activity is difficult and measuring voter contact even more so. The measures of contact used here are based on data that requires voters to recall whether and how they were contacted. The research creates a scale of contact, but the individual questions it draws on are binary (one leaflet counts the same as multiple leaflets), and it can't distinguish between work actually done locally and work delivered locally but directed centrally – mailshots and so on.

On the other hand, most voters will be unaware of whether a leaflet came through the door because an activist put it there or whether it was a paid-for mailshot. What matters is whether it looks like there is an active campaign. This may be an imprecise measure of that campaign, but it appears to be enough to capture changes in campaign viability. My assumption (no more than that) is that its imprecision probably understates the impact; a more precise measure might find even larger effects.

In short: if you go out in the wind and rain to fight the good fight, armed only with a pile of leaflets and a warm coat, you aren't wasting your time.

Further reading

J. Bochel and D. Denver, 'Canvassing, Turnout and Party Support: An Experiment', *British Journal of Political Science* (1971).

J. Fisher et al., 'Innocent Bystanders or the Forgotten Actors? The Role of Parties and Candidates in Building Electoral Campaign Momentum', *Political Studies* (2025).

CHAPTER 19

REALISM

We know a lot about what voters think of MPs. Much of it is not very positive. But what do MPs think about voters? Perhaps they take the view that voters are terribly well informed about politics, that the electorate eschew the short term and think about policies that will pay out in the long term, or that they think about the wider interests of the country rather than just looking out for themselves. They might think that voters have realistic expectations about what can be achieved by government, alert to the trade-offs and compromises involved in politics.

Or perhaps they don't.

There is no evidence that Winston Churchill ever actually said that the best argument against democracy was a five-minute conversation with the average voter. But you don't have to hang around politicians very long to hear some of them express similar sentiments.

Fascinating new research, recently published in the *American*

Political Science Review, examined the views of around 1,000 politicians in eleven countries and found that they were more likely to be sceptical about voters' capabilities and attitudes than optimistic. Many politicians had what the authors of the research describe as a 'thin, minimalist, relatively pessimistic view of voters' capacities'.

Some 73 per cent of respondents to their survey fall into a category they called 'democratic realists' – inspired by Christopher Achen and Larry Bartels's *Democracy for Realists,* a book which should be on everyone's reading list. There was a much smaller group of politicians who could be classified as democratic optimists (16 per cent). The remainder were undecided or inattentive.

The size of the more pessimistic group varied considerably by country and it is not immediately obvious what links the places where democratic realism is especially strong. Top of the pessimistic list was Czechia, where 83 per cent of politicians held such views, but not far behind were Canada, Israel and Belgium, and it's not clear – to me or to the authors of the paper – what links these four.

Ditto for places where politicians were less likely to be democratic pessimists. What links Denmark (the least pessimistic, at 54 per cent) with Switzerland, Australia and Sweden? Your guess is as good as mine.

But in all eleven countries studied, a majority of politicians held a pessimistic view of voters. Even in Denmark, democratic realist politicians outnumbered optimists by about two to one. In Czechia, it was ten to one.

The UK was not one of the eleven countries studied – a point to which I am going to return shortly.

The project also asked samples of voters the exact same questions, revealing that the electorate held a somewhat more optimistic view of their own capabilities. They were noticeably more likely than politicians were to be democratic optimists (34 per cent), although even among the electorate democratic realists were the single largest category (38 per cent), along with higher numbers who were undecided or inattentive. And while these numbers also varied from country to country, politicians were more likely to be democratic realists than voters in every country studied.

These broad categories were drawn from eight questions, tapping into central debates about electoral behaviour. Politicians and voters didn't differ on everything. Both, for example, saw voters as not especially knowledgeable about politics, with politicians no more likely to hold that view than voters, a finding that surprised me.

But on some questions, the differences were stronger. Politicians were more likely to think voters blamed politicians for events outside their control; they were more likely to think voters were short- rather than long-termist in their thinking; and they were more likely to think voters focused on single issues. These questions produced clear differences, fairly uniformly, across countries. Politicians were also more likely to think voters thought mostly about themselves rather being concerned for the good of the nation – egocentric rather than sociotropic in the jargon – and to think voters were more likely to be focused on leaders rather than ideas.

You might be wondering who is right. The answer is both that we don't know and that it doesn't hugely matter anyway. We don't know because these issues are all ongoing debates in electoral studies. Often there is no clear answer. Take political knowledge, for example. Some voters are knowledgeable about politics and policy, some quite spectacularly aren't. It can depend on what you are testing and how you measure it. Some voters have policy preferences that are sociotropic, some egocentric; some are sociotropic some of the time, egocentric the rest. It can vary by country and by context.

And it doesn't matter because what's more important is what politicians *think*. Perceptions are important, even if they are wrong. In the same way that what voters think about politics matters even if they are wrong, if politicians think voters are short-termist then they may behave accordingly – regardless of whether voters are or not.

I also find myself wondering whether these views change over time – are newly elected politicians more likely to be optimists, while older lags become pessimists? Or maybe these sorts of views are just in your blood. It would also be fascinating to see the study reversed one day: what do politicians and voters think about how politicians see the world? My assumption would be that we would see an almost exact mirror image, with political elites thinking they are long-termist and knowledgeable and voters thinking rather differently.

The findings are the latest to come out of a well-established, cross-national project, run out of the University of Antwerp, called POLPOP. It looks at how politicians see the world, comparing it to how things look through the eyes of the voters. The UK has not been one of the countries studied. Until now. The UK arm of POLPOP is launching this year. Invitations to participate in the next wave of questions will be arriving in MPs' inboxes throughout 2025. The realist me in fears they won't participate. The optimist in me hopes they do.

Further reading

C. Achen and L. Bartels, *Democracy for Realists* (2016).

J. Lucas et al., 'Politicians' Theories of Voting Behavior', *American Political Science Review* (2024).

CHAPTER 20

LOADSAMONEY

It is common these days to hear complaints about a lack of political engagement, so let me cheer you up by telling you about a demographic group where an astonishingly high one in nine of its members have sought political office. Let me introduce you to perhaps the most switched-on and politically active group of all. I am talking, of course, about billionaires.

The *Forbes* Billionaires List – the so-called 'three-comma club' – contains about 2,000 names. According to a fascinating recent study, just over 11 per cent of them have run for political office. It's difficult to think of any other group in society with that level of political ambition. Note that this 11 per cent figure is for those who have stood for elected office and excludes those involved in government in other ways; Elon Musk wouldn't count, for example. So, treat that 11 per cent as a minimum figure.

By political office we are, perhaps unsurprisingly, not talking service on the parish council. Billionaires tend to aim high. If they are going to be mayor, it's of New York, not Chigley. And in almost all cases, if they've sought office, they've held it. Of the 198 direct elections featuring billionaires that the researchers identified, the billionaire candidate won in 80 per cent – and they only managed to find eight billionaires who had sought office but ultimately failed. Imagine how that must sting for those eight?

Perhaps the most interesting finding, though, is *where* we find these mega-rich politicians. There are obvious examples from the US, such as Donald Trump or Michael Bloomberg, but mainland China alone accounted for over 110 of those identified – that's more than anywhere else, measured either in absolute terms or as a percentage of a country's billionaires. Hong Kong added twenty-one. Those two made up more than half the total cases identified. Indeed, given the opacity of wealth in China, the researchers argued that the true rate was probably higher and that this figure too should be treated as a minimum.

There were twenty-one such cases in the US, although one reason why the US has a lot of billionaire politicians is because it has a lot of billionaires – more than anywhere else in the world. Only around 4 per cent of them have sought political office, a figure that is just marginally higher than in many European countries. The relative rate is much higher in Russia and Singapore, which are both over 20 per cent.

Insofar as you can measure it, outside of China and especially in Europe, billionaires tend to lean towards the political right. You'd never have guessed.

There is an accompanying dataset called 'Billionaires in Politics Around the World', which allows you to play with the data if you are so inclined. You might well wonder if this is a sensible use of your time; the long winter evenings must just fly by, as Blackadder once put it. But it is surprisingly revealing.

For one thing, in about half of the countries that have produced billionaires, precisely none have sought political office. In other words, that 11 per cent figure is the worldwide average, but it is the product of a handful of countries with lots of mega-rich politicos and many more with very few or none.

Scan the list of British billionaires, for example, and you see plenty of familiar names: newspaper owners, party donors and so on. Many of them are influential; yet almost none of them have run for office. The dataset, based on the 2017 *Forbes* list, identifies just two British cases – the Barclay brothers, one of whom is now dead. Both are included due to their role in Sark, which is a pretty borderline and idiosyncratic case. Of the rest, nothing.

Yet in itself this is revealing. No one thinks that the Barclay brothers, who variously owned the *Daily Telegraph* and *The Scotsman*, weren't politically influential or involved in politics in a broader sense.

Compared to most other groups, that 11 per cent participation figure may be high, but maybe the interesting question is why it isn't higher. The very wealthy have a host of advantages politically. We often look at political recruitment in terms of the barriers due to cost of entry; for the mega-rich, the financial costs are a rounding error. They can donate large sums to their individual campaign or that of their party. And unsurprisingly perhaps, the research also found that over 12 per cent of billionaires had an ownership stake in a media company, which is always handy if running for office.

But once there, what's in it for them? Looking at the data, it's pretty clear that worldwide, billionaires tend to enter politics in large numbers where politics is a way of making or preserving money. That is not true in any significant way in most Western democracies. And anyway, billionaires can exercise influence in other ways. As the authors write: 'Extreme wealth provides ample opportunities to exert influence informally by funding candidates or parties with compatible policy preferences, shaping media narratives, and developing social ties and personal relationships with professional politicians.'

Billionaires can do all that without all the hassle of the formal political process. Who needs constituency surgeries every Friday in a draughty village hall? Formal involvement in the political process also brings with it enhanced scrutiny of the sort that may not always be welcome; this may be the real cost of entry.

One of the questions this research poses, therefore, is whether it would be better for *more* billionaires to run for office, especially in countries that require disclosure about politicians' conflicts of interest and financial affairs. Election would require billionaires to take and defend policy stances; it would involve some basic accountability. Sunlight, as the US Supreme Court Justice Louis Brandeis once claimed, is the best of disinfectants.

Further reading

D. Krcmaric et al., 'Billionaire Politicians: A Global Perspective', *Perspectives on Politics* (2024).

CHAPTER 21

PRESENCE

All the mainstream British political parties are, to varying degrees, signed up to the principle that political institutions should broadly reflect the social characteristics of the people they represent. In a groundbreaking book published in the 1990s, Anne Phillips referred to this as 'the politics of presence', as opposed to the politics of ideas.

This concern now encompasses a much wider range of social characteristics than it used to. For years, any politician discussing this subject would talk about the sex and (more recently) the ethnicity of MPs – and then there would be a slightly confused and vague reference to 'other groups', without it ever being clear who these other groups were.

But more recently these debates have included the representation of disability, sexuality, age and social class (the last, of course, being the original element of identity politics, albeit one that had been absent from discussion for decades). The scope of this politics of presence is currently wider than it had been at any point since mass suffrage was introduced.

One of the key arguments underpinning the politics of presence is that the type of people elected to Parliament – as opposed purely to their party label or political beliefs – is consequential. It leads to changes either within Parliament (different issues raised, different laws passed) or outside (as people become more engaged, people see politics as more for them and so on). Three recently published pieces of research demonstrate the latter neatly – and across four different characteristics. They also demonstrate that the effects are not always straightforward or predictable.

The first article, published in *Political Studies*, looks at representation of young people. It finds that as the percentage of young people in Parliament increases, so the gap between turnout of the young and the old at the ballot box narrows. The UK has some of the largest age-related turnout gaps seen in any of the nineteen Western European countries studied. In total, the paper examines turnout at fifty-seven elections; of the eleven largest turnout gaps, the UK is responsible for five of them.

Or take a second, equally intriguing finding, published in *Political Psychology*. In general, as more women are elected to Parliament, there is an increase in women's sense of political efficacy – the sense that they can influence politics. But using data from thirty-one OECD countries, the research finds that working-class and middle-class women react differently. Until female representation hits 20 per cent, there is no difference. But get past about 20 per cent and 'low-skilled workers are more likely than high-skilled workers to believe who is in power is irrelevant'.

The third article was published in the *American Political Science Review* and shows that the election of minority ethnic MPs to Westminster has the effect of boosting electoral turnout. Perhaps this is minority ethnic voters, previously disengaged with politics but now enthused by their new representative? Except that in this case, it appears that the turnout being boosted is primarily that of white voters, as part of a backlash against the election of a minority ethnic MP.

Using data from the four elections from 2010 to 2019, the research found that where a minority ethnic candidate won their seat against a white candidate, turnout in the subsequent election was some 4.3 percentage points higher than if the seat had been won by a white candidate. This difference holds only where the election is narrow (in other words where higher turnout next time might perhaps make a difference) and is driven by differences in white-majority constituencies. A supplementary, individual-level analysis of the behaviour of voters rather than of constituencies seems to confirm that this is a backlash against the election of non-white MPs.

When reading this sort of research, it's important to keep a sense of perspective. Even though youth turnout rises when young people are present in political institutions, young people are still on average less likely to participate in elections, even when their representation is high. Increased representation may reduce the problem of low youth participation; it does not remove it.

Similarly, even when the percentage of women in Parliament hits 45 per cent (which is true of precious few legislatures), the difference between the views of working-class and middle-class women is just 4 per cent. For the most part, increases in the number of women in Parliament leads to an increase in women's overall sense of political efficacy – just not as greatly among working-class women.

And while a 4.3 per cent rise in turnout isn't trivial, the definition of 'close' contests used in the backlash paper includes majorities of over 20 per cent; under half have a majority of 10 per cent or less. So even if all these voters came out for the second-placed candidate (and they wouldn't), they won't swing many seats. I also find myself wondering how long this effect lasts for. The research compares the result at one election with the next one (t+1, in the jargon). But by t+2 or +3? I suspect it will have evaporated.

Further reading

D. Angelucci et al., '"No Participation Without Representation": The Impact of Descriptive and Substantive Representation on the Age-Related Turnout Gap', *Political Studies* (2024).

Y. Kweon, 'We see symbols but not saviors: Women's representation and the political attitudes of working-class women', *Political Psychology* (2024).

S. Zonszein and G. Grossman, 'Turnout Turnaround: Ethnic Minority Victories Mobilize White Voters', *American Political Science Review* (2023).

CHAPTER 22

LEAFLETS

For all the changes in political campaigning in recent years, the main method of direct contact between the parties and the British voter remains the humble leaflet or letter pushed through someone's front door, usually by a party activist or supporter.

You wouldn't know this from much of the coverage of elections. You will have to look hard to find any discussion in the media about a party's leaflets. It's all a bit too retro. Not shiny and new enough.

There's no doubt that digital campaigning is growing in importance, election-on-election, but when discussing election campaigns, it is worth always remembering Deep Throat's advice to 'follow the money'. Of around £50 million spent nationally by the parties in 2019, the biggest single category of expenditure, some £20 million, went on what the Electoral Commission call 'unsolicited material to electors' – leaflets, direct mail and so on.

A much more detailed analysis of the almost 23,000 items of expenditure from 2019 logged with the Electoral Commission was recently published in *Government and Opposition* and it found something very similar. It involved back-breaking research work, with a team of coders ploughing through invoice after invoice. If you are wondering why there is no equivalent analysis of the 2024 contest, just imagine how long it takes to go through that many invoices.

The researchers found that the vast majority of expenditure in 2019 went on campaign activities that would have been very familiar to anyone campaigning in the 1980s or even much earlier. Yes, there was evidence of online campaigning, social media promotion, mobile apps, data analytics and so on. But these were blended with – and in terms of expenditure, secondary to – much more old-fashioned campaign techniques. Under a fifth of election expenditure in 2019 went on campaigning techniques dating from 2008 or later.

'I have never understood why journalists don't focus on leaflets more,' a party staffer once said to me. 'If you want to know what our message is, look at what we're putting through people's doors.' In surveys of voters, it is the leaflet or letter – respondents are not great at differentiating between the two – that gets noticed the most. Everything else is secondary.

This has prompted me, only slightly tongue in cheek, to formulate Cowley's Law of Election Campaigns: there is an inverse relationship between the importance of any election campaign technique and the amount of media coverage devoted to it.

Hence why I was interested in another newly published piece

of research examining what form of communication voters preferred. Drawing on data from the 2016 Welsh Senedd elections, it asked people what they had noticed receiving from the parties – and once again, leaflets were top by a long way (36 per cent). Below that you had telephone calls (8 per cent), being canvassed at home (4 per cent) and personal letters (2 per cent). Fewer than 2 per cent of electors said they were contacted by either email or social media platforms such as Twitter/X or Facebook.

It's worth being a bit cautious about these numbers in absolute terms. Self-reporting almost certainly underestimates levels of contact. Even in the most marginal constituencies in general elections, for example, in which every voter will have received multiple communications from the parties, the percentage of these communications reported is always remarkably low. My suspicion is that some forms of contact are especially likely to go unnoticed: people remember the more active (canvassing, phone calls) but perhaps overlook or forget the more passive (leaflets or social media, where they might see something online without realising it has come from a political party). Still, the differences are striking.

The researchers then asked what form of communication people *wanted* from the parties, the first time I have ever seen this question asked.

Turns out about a third said that they didn't want to be contacted at all. It's common to hear voters complain of politicians that 'we never see them around here apart from at elections'. For a third of voters, the reality is 'we never see them around here and that's the way we like it'.

But of those who said they did want to hear from the parties, top came leaflets – the preferred choice of just under a third of respondents. There was then a sizeable gap before any of the other methods of contact: 11 per cent said email and home visits and 9 per cent said personal letters, with e-campaigning methods coming in at 3 per cent.

As the authors wrote: 'The data suggest that there remains a strong demand among electors to be contacted by traditional campaign activities such as leaflets and canvassing.'

They noted what they described as 'considerable heterogeneity in voters' contact methods' – or in other words, people differ in how they'd like parties to talk to them. Older voters, for example, were keener on doorstep conversations than the young, with younger voters more likely to prefer e-campaigning than those older.

Yet the heterogeneity wasn't all that considerable. Both these groups preferred leaflets over everything else. Indeed, based on what was reported in the paper, it looks as if the leaflet was the preferred contact method for almost every group of voters. Voters are much more old school than is often realised.

This isn't a call for parties to dump alternate campaigning methods. All have their virtues, and in practice, campaigns aren't about choosing one or the other. Horses for courses and all that.

But we'd do well to remember Willie Sutton. He was the bank

robber who when asked why he robbed banks, reputedly replied: 'Because that's where the money is.' Journalists covering elections should do the same. Go where the parties are devoting their money and efforts and report that.

Further reading

K. Dommett et al., 'Understanding the Modern Election Campaign: Analysing Campaign Eras through Financial Transparency Disclosures at the 2019 UK General Election', *Government and Opposition* (2024).

J. Townsley and D. Cutts, 'How Do Voters Want to be Contacted and Are Parties Listening? Evidence from a Recent Election in Wales', *Political Studies* (2023).

CHAPTER 23

DATA

Many years ago, as a postgraduate student, my friend Dave had the idea of looking at backbench rebellions in what are now called public bill committees – the committees that examine the detail of pieces of legislation in the House of Commons.

All the information he needed was public, in that it was printed and available, at least in major libraries. But none of it was online or searchable in any meaningful way. So, he sat in the university's parliamentary papers room in silence, turning page after page of volume after volume of Commons records, looking for those occasions where there had been a vote.

Periodically, he'd find one. He'd stop turning the pages and quickly scan the list of names of the MPs involved. Usually, everyone had voted the same way. But every now and again, someone had broken ranks. He'd say: 'Got one.' I would smile, in a way I hoped was encouraging rather than weird, and he'd go back to turning the pages again in silence. Very occasionally, maybe once or twice a day, he'd find a rebellion where enough MPs had rebelled to mean the government were defeated and we'd head off to the library cafe for a coffee or a doughnut to celebrate.

In total, over that summer, Dave looked at the 5,306 standing committee divisions that took place between 1979 and 1992. He found a total of 684 dissenting votes by Conservative MPs, spread across 103 bills, inflicting fifty-six defeats.

For some strange reason, Dave decided that this wasn't the way he wanted to spend the rest of his life and after graduating, he went to get a proper job.

I didn't – and have been studying the way MPs vote for about thirty years. What a loser. But then, you're reading a book written by someone who studies the way MPs vote, so you're in no position to mock, are you?

Every now and again, I think I might try to do something else, but it proves difficult to get away. Like Al Pacino in *The Godfather Part III*, just when you think you're out, they pull you back in again. There's always MPs grumpy about something; there's always a minister about to do something daft and MPs trying to stop them. The downside of writing about this sort of stuff is that it's contemporary and you have to run to keep up. But that's the upside too.

I was reminded of Dave recently when reading a new piece of research examining the representation of women from 'minoritised groups', a phrase deliberately designed to include religion as well as ethnicity.

The finding was interesting in itself: minoritised female MPs were almost seven times more likely to discuss the issues of minoritised women in Parliament than were white male MPs. Plus, when they did so, they were more likely to raise a much broader set of concerns. The research was yet another example of the extent to which the identity of MPs affects how they behave.

Of just as much interest – and the reason it reminded me of that summer spent in the library – was the process. This new paper drew on a dataset of 1.1 million speeches in the Commons over the twenty-year period between 1997 and 2017, all downloadable at a click of a button or two. This enabled analysis on a scale and with an ease that would have been unimaginable to the two of us sat there day after day, turning the pages of Hansard.

This isn't a one-off either. The digitisation of parliamentary records has facilitated a mini-explosion of research like this, examining those aspects of parliamentary behaviour where a lot of the action takes place – things like parliamentary questions or speeches – but where the logistics of large-scale research were previously often prohibitive. There's a handful of examples in this book, but I could easily have done a book just on these sorts of studies.

It still takes work to get the data in a usable form (as anyone who has done it will tell you, the reality is never just the click of a button or two) and human intervention is often still required. In this particular case, having found some 37,729 sentences containing possible mentions of minoritised women, the researcher then examined each one herself to see if they were genuine and should be included in her analysis or spurious and needed rejecting. (Yes, you read that right: 37,729.) But the growth of AI should make even this easier, reducing the costs of research yet further.

It's not all positive. There are cases where this relative ease has produced research that misses something obvious, something that would have been clear to anyone who had spent any decent amount of time with the original source material. The very ease of access to the data can result in the researcher failing to understand what it is they are examining. It would be unfair of me to single out any such studies by name and they are, thankfully, a minority – but they are more common than they should be. Turning the pages had its virtues.

Let's not wear a hair shirt, though. For the most part, all the time we used to spend just gathering information can be better spent analysing it. That's worth a doughnut or two.

Further reading

D. Melhuish and P. Cowley, 'Whither the "new role" in policy making? Conservative MPs in standing committees, 1979 to 1992', *Journal of Legislative Studies* (1995).

O. Siow, 'Needles in a haystack: an intersectional analysis of the descriptive, constitutive and substantive representation of minoritized women', *European Journal of Politics and Gender* (2023).

CHAPTER 24

SCUM

The report by the Electoral Commission into the 2024 general election made depressing reading. Some 70 per cent of the candidates who responded to their survey reported some abuse or harassment; a third said they were intimidated or deliberately made to feel unsafe at least once during the campaign. A majority of candidates said that they avoided some form of campaign activity due to fear of abuse. Women and those from minority ethnic backgrounds reported the highest levels of abuse.

Have you ever wondered about those who dish it out?

Fascinating new research looked at the public's attitudes to abusing politicians. If you are a politician, then the good news here is that the public mostly thought it wasn't acceptable.

Using a standard representative survey, the researchers asked about six different types of behaviour, including sending abusive emails, making physical threats or daubing slogans on offices or homes.

Measured on a seven-point scale (from 'not at all' to 'entirely'), on the question of whether it was ever acceptable to visit a politician's office and threaten them physically, 90 per cent gave a score of zero, the lowest possible.

The most acceptable activity seemed to be sending insulting emails, where 38 per cent gave a score of zero. But even here, once you add in those who gave scores of one or two – that is, also on the not-acceptable side of the scale – you reached 78 per cent.

Many of the researchers' attempts to discover differences in the *type* of people who were more tolerant of abuse produced null findings. There was relatively little difference between the political right or left, for example. There was little evidence of polarisation mattering; if anything, centrists were more tolerant of abuse. Women are slightly less abusive than men, although the differences were pretty small – and, for some reason, women think it's more OK to send an insulting email than men. There were some signs that populists or those with sexist attitudes were more tolerant of abuse, but even then, the majority were not and the differences were not massive.

Overall, the authors saw the work as something to be upbeat about. They wrote: 'Only small fractions of the British public think that intimidation or aggression against politicians is anything other than completely unacceptable. Sending an insulting email may be understandable, but there is almost universal strong condemnation of the most threatening forms of abuse.'

I'm a little less sanguine. There's a Wodehouse line about the fascination of shooting as a sport depending almost wholly on whether you are at the right or wrong end of the gun. I suspect that whether these percentages seem big or small probably depends a lot on whether you are the one likely to be on the receiving end of them.

In percentage terms, large majorities were against abuse, but in absolute terms, the minorities are still sizeable. Take the 12 per cent who think that it is OK to send an insulting email; that represents 6 million people and enough to make MPs' inboxes pretty unpleasant. There may only be 2 per cent who think it is OK to visit an office and make physical threats, but that's still over 1,500 people per constituency. Given that two MPs have been murdered at constituency events in the past ten years, this is not an abstract concern for politicians.

I was also struck by a second question that was asked, about whether such behaviour was *understandable*. As with the question about acceptability, the majority, and often a large majority, felt the various types of abuse were not understandable. Yet the percentage thinking such behaviour was understandable was always higher than the percentage who thought it was acceptable.

Take, for example, the question about painting insulting slogans on an MP's home. Some 82 per cent of people answered with a score of zero when asked if that was acceptable; 97 per cent were in the 0–2 range. The equivalent figures for whether the same behaviour was understandable were 64 per cent and

90 per cent. Some 17 per cent thought it was understandable that people might visit a politician's office and shout insults; over a third gave a score of 4 to 6 when asked if sending insulting emails was understandable. You have to wonder whether this is a better gauge of whether the behaviour really is seen as beyond the pale. If you think something is understandable, do you really think it's not acceptable? *Tout comprendre, c'est tout pardonner* and all that.

Plus, there was a clear age gradient. The younger the respondents, the more they were in favour of abusing politicians. The consequences of this will depend on whether this is a generational effect or a life-cycle effect. If the latter and if it's something young people grow out of, like a belief in fairies or Santa Claus, then it's no big deal. But if it's the former, then things are about to get worse. Either way, there's no indication they're going to get better.

One wonders if those who dish it out could take it. Alas, I suspect the spoilsports on the university's Ethics Committee would look askance at this idea – but imagine if anyone who responded to a survey saying that it's OK to send abusive emails to MPs got sent one themselves. 'Thanks for taking part in our survey, you dickhead.' Those who think it's OK to paint abuse on an MP's home could wake up the next morning to find that someone's sprayed their garage door with the word SCUM. Let's see how they like it.

Further reading

Electoral Commission, 'Report on the 2024 UK Parliamentary general election and the May 2024 elections' (2024).

S. Shair-Rosenfield et al., 'Who Tolerates Abuse of MPs?', *Political Insight* (2024).

CHAPTER 25

WHATEVER

I n October 1924, the spinal specialist Clement Jeffery gave a lecture at Mortimer Hall on the subject of 'nerves'. He advised his audience to avoid talking about politics before going to bed. 'All such disputations,' he said, 'produce bad temper, disturb sleep and tend to exhaust the nervous system.'

He added that frequent general elections were, from the strictly physiological standpoint, 'disastrous to the nervous stability of politicians in particular and the public generally'. (Amen to that.) A week later, in another talk, he advised those going out to vote to skip a meal to increase their mental faculties when in the polling station.

Mr Jeffery was a man with no shortage of theories; already, in the same year, he had argued that the recent transport strikes would see the demise of the high heel and that horn-rimmed glasses were the cause of the nation's ocular crisis.

It is never good to speak ill of the dead, but now that he is no longer with us, it seems safe to say that, methodologically speaking, his work does seem to have had more than a whiff of the approach known as Making It Up as You Go Along. He did, however, seem to be very good at gaining widespread media coverage, off the back of some strongly held opinions and not a lot of evidence. It's a good job we don't have academics like that these days.

Which doesn't necessarily mean – high heels notwithstanding – that he was entirely wrong. For example, I recently read an article about the 2020 US election, which showed that caring about elections did indeed affect your emotional status. Overall, Joe Biden's election in 2020 had had the effect of lowering levels of political anxiety among American voters. Yet the effect was not uniform and those who were highly politically engaged or interested in politics were more anxious after the election than those who had tuned out. When it comes to politics: don't worry, be happy.

On an entirely unrelated subject – but then again, perhaps not – I also recently read a paper looking at how American voters reacted to politicians who had been accused of sexual misconduct. It involved a survey experiment, which asked respondents to consider a hypothetical candidate, from the same party as they supported, who was running for governor. The same party bit is important: it's easy to condemn someone from the other lot, easy to find excuses when it is one of your own.

The researchers split their sample into two. Half of respondents were shown some boilerplate information about the candidate;

the other half were told that he had been accused of sexual harassment and had settled out of court.

Perhaps unsurprisingly, the allegations had an electoral cost – being told about the harassment allegations lowered the probability of voting for the candidate by 51 per cent. But the neat bit about this particular study is that it asked those who were still prepared to back the guy *why* they were prepared to do so.

The most common justification was what is called 'moral licensing' – where, to quote from the paper, 'past good deeds can liberate individuals to engage in behaviours that are immoral, unethical, or otherwise problematic'. That accounted for just under half of the respondents. As one survey participant said: 'I think what he has done for the state in the past should speak loudly.'

The second most common strategy was straightforward disbelief; over a quarter of respondents dismissed the allegations as fake news or similar. In part, this was about the court case – 'It's not just a matter of being accused and settling out of court. That doesn't imply anything at all except to stupid people.' – but there was also a wider scepticism about those who make allegations against politicians ('They're just trying to extort money; they should have come forward at the time.')

And then there were some outright partisans. As one put it: 'I'm assuming that it's a battle between this guy who sounds like a Democrat and a criminal Republican. In this case, I have no choice.' He may be a sexual predator, their argument seemed to be, but at least he's *our* sexual predator.

What I find really striking about this study is not these arguments themselves but that this effect manifested itself in response to an entirely hypothetical scenario. In a real-world case, with flesh and blood candidates and bona fide policy outcomes, you could well imagine all sorts of moral compromises manifesting themselves. Doing the right thing in the real world often has a cost and the better angels of our nature don't always emerge triumphant.

But here, asked about a literal paper candidate and with no consequences whatsoever, you could give the socially desirable 'right' answer entirely cost-free. It's why the size of effects discovered in experiments like this are often larger than we see in the real world when politicians face actual scandals – if real-world politicians who had settled out of court suffered a 51 per cent electoral penalty, there wouldn't be very many of them left.

Yet still plenty of people did not give the socially desirable right answer. Maybe these people were just being more honest?

Further reading

M. Savani and S. Collignon, 'Moral licence and disbelief: how voters look past political misconduct', *Political Research Exchange* (2024).

K. Smith et al., 'On pins and needles: anxiety, politics and the 2020 U.S. Presidential election', *Journal of Elections, Public Opinion and Parties* (2023).

CHAPTER 26

VISITS

In June 2024, with the election in full swing, Keir Starmer took part in a photocall at the Memorial Stadium in Bristol. This brought together Bristol Rovers and the Labour Party, the two organisations that did more than any others to disappoint my late father during his time on this earth. Dying a few months later, he lived long enough to cheer Labour's landslide, but he never did get to see an FA Cup and league-winning double.

Advance teams, those who scout out possible venues for events like this, are one of the many unsung heroes of election campaigns. Living for weeks on the road, surviving on take-aways and Premier Inn breakfasts, trying to persuade venues to do things they don't want to ('Can we shut down your business for a day and stop you making money?'), they aim to ensure that the leaders' events go off smoothly and they are not – with luck – photographed near too many exit signs or similar. Extreme caution needs to be taken with events in Scunthorpe.

Does any of it matter, though? A fascinating paper, recently published in *Political Studies*, finds that the answer is maybe, a little. The authors examined more than 600 campaign stops taken by the Labour, Conservative and Lib Dem leaders during the four general elections from 2010 to 2019. Focusing just on England, they find distinctly patchy results. Many events take place in marginal seats but lots do not. For some parties, local campaign expenditure seems important; for others, not as much.

The authors split leaders' visits into four types. Two were essentially outward-facing: grandstanding events (formal speeches and such like) and what they call policy-orientated events, using the local setting to make some general point (a photo op at a hospital designed to show how much the party cares about health policy, for example). Two were more inward-facing: campaigning events, where the leader does a walkabout in a town centre or goes canvassing with a local candidate, or cheerleader events, where the leader gives a rally for local party supporters.

The policy-orientated event is the most common; it was the most common type at each of the four elections. In 2010, over three-quarters of Nick Clegg's visits were classified as policy-orientated, the most of any of the leaders studied. The most grandstanding? Ed Miliband in 2015. The most campaigning? Jeremy Corbyn in 2017, when 46 per cent of his visits were campaigning trips. Yet two years later, Corbyn's figure had dropped to just 16 per cent and he was instead the most likely to cheerlead, which accounted for 57 per cent of his visits at the 2019 election. Much depends on who the leader is but also, as the example of Corbyn shows, the political context in which they find themselves.

The results are that leaders' visits do produce small electoral benefits – although a visit by Nick Clegg in 2015 seems to have been enough to put voters off the Lib Dems – but the effects really are tiny. Perhaps this is just as well. If we found that a twenty-minute photo op in which a party leader and a group of nursery schoolchildren played with modelling clay was sufficient to sway large numbers of voters, then we would perhaps want to reconsider the world's experiment with democracy.

But I also think there is an issue in how we might go about measuring this. This piece of research uses the constituency as the unit of analysis. But many visits will have a much wider impact.

Let's return to that Memorial Stadium visit in June. The ground is to be found in Bristol North West. Do we think that when pictures appeared on the evening news, voters in Bristol East took umbrage? 'That Keir Starmer, he doesn't care about folk like us, he's only interested in that lot in Bristol North West.' Or do we think it's more likely that – lacking detailed knowledge of constituency boundaries – for most Bristolians, the visit instead ticked a box marked Labour Leader Visits My City.

As it happens, things are made even more complicated in this case by boundary changes. The Memorial Stadium used to be in Bristol West, a constituency that was abolished ahead of the 2024 contest. (Fun fact: of the ninety-two football league grounds in

England and Wales, it was the one in the most pro-Remain constituency.) That particular photo op was attended by the former MP for Bristol West, who was now standing in Bristol Central. All very confusing. Either way, insofar as any voters were moved by it, it seems unlikely that the impact would have stopped at the constituency border.

This, I think, helps to explain the slightly dampened effect. Of course, for some events, the precise constituency will really matter, but for others perhaps much less – and what will matter is hitting local media networks. The assumption of this particular research is that these visits should be seen as part of the constituency battle. They might be better off seen as part of the election air war – and especially the regional air war.

This is a part of the election battlefield that often goes unnoticed: local drive-time radio, op-eds in regional papers, local BBC and ITV news and similar. Such outlets are often missing from accounts of elections. My assumption is that this is because such accounts are often written by either big-name journalists who mostly work for, and think about, national-level media or by academics, who mostly don't listen to local news either. All too provincial and infra dig.

Further reading

D. Cutts and A. Middleton, 'Where Do They Go and Why, How Do They Vary and What Is Their Impact: Assessing Leaders' Campaign Visits in England 2010–2019', *Political Studies* (2024).

CHAPTER 27

PMQS

Prime Minister's Question Time began as a regular fixed slot in the parliamentary schedule in 1961. It is simultaneously the most high-profile and widely criticised part of parliamentary life. Periodically, there are pledges to change its culture and make it less adversarial, but this never lasts and behaviour always reverts to type. To be upfront about my own biases, I can't stand it – I only watch when obliged and always feel slightly dirty afterwards.

Yet the evidence that it is harmful to the reputation or standing of Parliament – as frequently claimed – is remarkably slim. The last Speaker used to complain that he received 'bucket loads' of letters complaining about the behaviour of MPs, yet when his correspondence on the subject was released, it became clear it was a fairly small bucket: about six letters per session of PMQs.

A fascinating piece of research recently placed PMQs into context, comparing behaviour in the UK with that in Australia, Canada and Ireland, all of which have plenary sessions in which the Prime Minister can be directly questioned. These all have varying procedures and practices, which produce different types of behaviour, but it is striking that the UK does not come out as the worst-behaved, whichever measure of conflict is analysed.

Take, for example, the extent to which the Speaker intervenes to call for order, challenge the nature of questions or expel members. Out of the four parliaments studied, the Australian one comes out the worst-behaved – with an average of 12.8 interventions by the Speaker in every session of questions. Ireland came a distant second (3.2 interventions per session), the UK third (2.5). That Australians play politics rough is perhaps not the most novel research discovery, but some of the figures are still remarkable: these interventions included thirty-nine cases of ordering people from the Chamber. The other three parliaments totalled zero expulsions.

The research also examined the nature of the questions asked. Slightly to my surprise, Canada, not perhaps known for its adversarial politics, came top, with close to 80 per cent of questions there being conflictual in nature, whereas the figures for the UK and Australia were nearer 40 per cent. Ah, you may say, but I bet in those countries parliamentarians focused their attacks on policy, rather than the partisan or ad hominem stuff that dominates PMQs. I bring bad news. In all four cases, the vast majority of conflictual questions focused on personalities and parties, not policy.

This research examined one premiership in each country

– the UK data drew on 2010–15 – and over time the precise nature of the figures will doubtless differ (different Speakers, different party leaders, different circumstances and so on), but one general conclusion seems clear. If you have an open, plenary session in which the Prime Minister can be questioned, it will be adversarial and conflictual. It might differ in exactly which bits are conflictual or how – in the UK, for example, most of the Speaker's interventions were about what the paper calls 'contextual conflict' (poor behaviour, heckling and so on), whereas in Ireland most were about the content of the questions being asked. But conflict in some form seems to be ever-present. It is a feature, not a bug.

And maybe it's a positive feature. For all that the theatrics of PMQs are criticised, other research has shown that parliaments with these sorts of adversarial exchanges have *higher* levels of political engagement among voters than those that do not. Based on analysis in sixteen counties, a study from 2014 found that not only was voter turnout higher in countries where there were open and quick-fire question times but also that voters there were more knowledgeable about politics. These findings held after controlling for other factors such as the age or class of voters or the type of political system.

And another piece of experimental research in which respondents were shown clips from PMQs to test their reactions found that while people didn't especially like what they saw, exposure to PMQs did not reduce their satisfaction with politics and could in fact boost 'internal efficacy' (that is, people's levels of confidence in their political comprehension).

Some caution is needed here. For example, when comparing countries, it is always possible that there is some other variable, not tested, that explains the apparent difference. I would want to see a bit more research before I became convinced that it really was PMQs driving those higher levels of engagement. And with experimental work it is always difficult to know whether the sort of effects one finds in a one-off experiment would last in the real world – what's called external validity. This particular study reported the effects of watching one three-minute clip of PMQs. Maybe that is positive, but maybe repeated exposure would produce a different outcome – in the same way that while one McDonald's might not turn you into a porker, you would be ill-advised to make it the cornerstone of your diet.

But still, these are far from the negative sort of results that we might expect, given how PMQs is usually discussed. It's often dismissed as Punch and Judy politics, but people did at least want to watch Punch and Judy – perhaps better that than to be dull?

The authors of the experimental paper concluded that the positive effects may be 'because the drama of PMQs commands attention, prompting viewers to be more fully engaged than they otherwise might be while viewing more civil legislative discourse'. They found there was no obvious difference between the partisanship of the respondents, although an individual's own personality type did make a difference, with those who were more favourable towards disagreement in general reacting more positively. 'For those who like that sort of thing,' as Miss Jean Brodie said, 'that is the sort of thing they like.'

Further reading

A. Convery et al., 'Questioning scrutiny: the effect of Prime Minister's Questions on citizen efficacy and trust in parliament', *Journal of Legislative Studies* (2021).

R. Salmond, 'Parliamentary Question Times: How Legislative Accountability Mechanisms Affect Mass Political Engagement', *Journal of Legislative Studies* (2014).

R. Serban, 'Conflictual behaviour in legislatures: Exploring and explaining adversarial remarks in oral questions to prime ministers', *British Journal of Politics and International Relations* (2023).

CHAPTER 28

AND

The concept of geographic representation is central to almost all representative systems. Most parliaments are organised around the representation of distinct geographic areas – constituencies, wards, districts, ridings or similar – and for the most part citizens are represented by where they live. Parliamentary constituencies in the UK are named after the areas they cover. This distinguishes them from, say, those in the US House of Representatives (1st Congressional District, 2nd Congressional District and so on) or the Australian House of Representatives (which are mostly named after people).

The bad news is that the constituency names currently in use are the longest and most cumbersome since Britain first began to use single-member, one-person, one-vote constituencies in 1950.

In 1950, for example, the average constituency title was 12.8 characters long. By 2019, it had hit 15.1. The current names weigh in at 17.1.

In 1950, just 14 per cent of constituency names contained

twenty or more characters; the equivalent figure for 2010 was 26 per cent. The figure for those now in use is 36 per cent.

Constituency names comprising just one word ('Gower', 'Westbury', 'Ayr' and so on) are in decline. In the 1950s, over 40 per cent of constituency seat names consisted of a single word; in 2019, that was true of just over 30 per cent. It has now fallen to 23 per cent.

Relatedly, there has been a noticeable rise in the use of the dread word 'and' (as in 'Windsor and Maidenhead' or 'Moray and Nairn'), linking two (and sometimes more) communities. In 1950, this applied to just fifty-three constituencies. In 2019 it applied to 161. Of the names now in use, a full 250 constituencies have 'and' somewhere in their title.

In other words, in 1950 'and' featured in under 10 per cent of constituency names. It features in over a third now – and, for the first time, we have more constituencies with 'and' in their title than there are constituency names consisting of a single word.

There have long been clear differences by nation. Scottish constituency names are longer than anywhere else in the UK (an average of 21.7 characters), which has been true since 1950, but at least in the recent boundary changes we lost 'Cumbernauld, Kilsyth and Kirkintilloch East', which holds the post-1950 record for the longest title. Constituency names in Wales used to be noticeably shorter than elsewhere in the UK but have grown in length over time and exceeded those in Northern Ireland, where the growth has been less dramatic, in 1997.

But constituency names have grown everywhere between 1950 and 2010. This prolixity is being driven by two factors: one is top-down, the other bottom-up.

The top-down pressure is that boundary redistributions in the UK have increasingly come to prioritise creating seats consisting of (roughly) equal electorates over the desire for seats that represent actual communities. In their book on boundary commissions, David Rossiter and his colleagues called this the tension between the organic and the mathematic principles of representation.

The law now explicitly prioritises the mathematic over the organic. It has placed much stricter limits on the extent to which constituencies can vary in terms of number of voters; with a handful of exceptions, seats must now be within 5 per cent of the average. All other things being equal, constituencies named after organic communities might be expected to have shorter, easier names than those where prioritising the mathematic principle leads to a need to create constituencies out of multiple different areas, all with their own identities. With this desire for arithmetic equality has come more lumping together of distinct communities and the creation of far more seats of the 'X and Y' (or even 'X, Y and Z') variety.

The second factor is that the process of boundary redistribution now includes greater public participation. Constituency names are a frequent source of dispute at public hearings. Boundary commissions have in the past been relatively relaxed about agreeing to changes in nomenclature, seeing it as a relatively easy way to demonstrate being consultative without having to make substantive changes to a seat in a way that would have knock-on effects on other constituencies.

You can see this happening in real time by comparing multiple versions of the seats proposed in the most recent boundary changes. In the Commission's original proposals, there were 209 seats with 'and' in the title; that rose to 224 by the time of their revised proposals and hit 250 by the final ones. The average length similarly went up, from 15.8 to 16.4 to 17.1.

In other words, of the overall increase from the average length of 15.1 characters in use in 2019, around 0.7 points can be attributed to the new legal framework and 1.3 points to the public consultation.

Does this issue require immediate ministerial action? Probably not. Is it perhaps the nerdiest thing you've ever read? More likely. When some of these stats were first published, a piece in *The Spectator* argued that anyone who cared about such things must have had their heads flushed down the toilet one too many times at school – before adding 'or perhaps not often enough'. No comment.

But still, it is worth considering at what point constituency names become too cumbersome to be easily or accurately used. The mean average length creeping up by a character or two probably does not matter very much, but the increasing use of multi-word constituencies, often involving two or three distinct places, can reduce their practical value.

Do these longer titles get used, in full and accurately, or are they just abbreviated or mangled? If the latter is the case – and anecdotally, it seems to be – then perhaps we should at least attempt to keep their number to a bare minimum.

Further reading

P. Cowley and M. Bailey, 'What's in a Name? The Length of Westminster Constituency Titles, 1950–2024', *Political Quarterly* (2021).

D. Rossiter et al., *The Boundary Commissions. Redrawing the UK's Map of Parliamentary Constituencies* (1999).

CHAPTER 29

PMs

W̶ho was the most successful Prime Minister? Asked to grade the post-war Prime Ministers on a range from 0 ('highly unsuccessful') to 10 ('highly successful'), one recent study of MPs' views – published shortly before the 2024 election – saw Margaret Thatcher come top, with an average response of 7.8. Not far behind came Clement Attlee and Tony Blair (both 7.4).

These rankings can wax and wane as reputations change. Compare the latest scores to a similar survey by the same project in 2013. Ten years before, Gordon Brown was bottom out of twelve. He's the biggest climber in the past decade, now ninth out of sixteen. Yet the top three have remained identical and most scores have not changed very much.

The responses are unsurprisingly often driven by partisan bias (but then who among us isn't?) Labour MPs graded Labour PMs more positively; the same, *mutatis mutandis*, for the Conservatives. The largest intra-party difference came with Thatcher, where Conservative MPs graded her on average at 9.2, Labour at 6.4. Ask the Tories and the best post-war PMs were Thatcher, Churchill and Cameron, in that order, with Macmillan and Blair tying for fourth. For Labour MPs, the top PMs were Blair, Attlee and Wilson, with Brown and Thatcher joint fourth.

Given the radically different partisan mix in the House, if the survey was redone today, it would almost certainly see Thatcher do less well and Attlee and Blair better. That said, there was cross-party consensus about those at the bottom. Anthony Eden, who always used to be the go-to reference if you wanted to discuss someone who made a mess of things, scored 3.2. But now we have Liz Truss, who scored 0.7; among Labour MPs, she averaged 0.1.

Winning general elections does not guarantee being seen as a successful Prime Minister, although the multiple-election victors scored better on average than those who won a single victory; in turn, the single-election winners scored better than the PMs who never managed to win a contest. Length of tenure also mattered. There was a clear correlation between the length of time spent in No. 10 and the mean score. Longevity wasn't everything, but it's difficult to be a success if you are not there for very long – although it turns out it's possible to be a failure in quite a short period of time.

Missing from the analysis, I think, was size of majority – or at least the presence of a solid majority. The three top Prime Ministers in the league table all enjoyed landslide majorities for significant periods of their premierships. Again, this doesn't ensure success – there were plenty of Prime Ministers with large majorities who polled much worse, a list that includes Liz Truss – but it does facilitate it.

The survey also included a question about the characteristics required to be a successful Prime Minister. Top of the list came being decisive. Yet it is very difficult to be decisive without a decent majority. We can pray in aid John Major here, who sits comfortably mid-table in the rankings but who knew, more than most, the difficulties of governing without a comfortable majority. In 1993, some off-the-record remarks he made to a journalist were leaked, in which he appeared to describe three members of his Cabinet as bastards. But they were not what he identified as his core problem. 'The real problem,' he said, 'is one of a tiny majority… I could have all these clever, decisive things which people wanted me to do, but I would have split the Conservative party into smithereens. And you would have said I had acted like a ham-fisted leader'.

There is one other aspect of the research that was interesting, if depressing for those of us on this side of the parliament– academic divide. The latest paper is based on responses from sixty-five MPs. That is, 10 per cent of the House. When the researchers did their earlier study ten years before, they had a response rate of around 25 per cent.

Just like a survey of the public, MPs can be sampled – we don't need everybody to have replied – but there can come a point at which a sample becomes too small. This paper made efforts to check that their respondents were broadly representative (which they were) and the results are in line with other surveys, but it speaks to a wider issue: it is getting harder and harder to survey parliamentarians.

I understand why. Politicians are busy people with an almost infinite set of demands on their time. While some people might be flattered to be asked to take part in an academic study, politicians generally are not. They get bombarded with requests from schoolkids, university students, lecturers, pressure groups and various randoms. If they said yes to everyone, they'd spend their entire day doing nothing else but filling in surveys or giving interviews. Plus, there's always a risk that it's not a genuine project with anonymity guaranteed (as this one was) but an attempt to stitch them up. Why risk it?

A similar problem applies to those who want to interview MPs. I owe my career to the kindness of hundreds of MPs who gave up their time to talk to me. But colleagues tell me this too is getting harder. It's all a long way from the 1970s, when Donald Searing's study (discussed in Chapter 16) managed to interview 521 MPs (an 83 per cent response rate), with face-to-face interview times ranging from thirty minutes to an astonishing five hours.

But this should worry MPs too. They are becoming harder to reach by researchers at the same time as quantitative data about their behaviour is becoming increasingly easily available. With relatively little effort, I can now track how an MP is voting, or what questions they are asking or how often they are turning up to a select committee.

This runs the risk of research being based purely on observable behaviour and lacking the rounded understanding of the institution that you can only get from asking people questions, whether it's face to face or via questionnaires. Anyone who knows anything about Parliament knows that the observable data only gets you so far. If you want to really understand the place, you do need to be able to talk to people. It's in MPs' own interests not to put the survey straight in the bin.

Further reading

Royal Holloway Group PR3710, 'The good, the not so good, and Liz Truss: MPs' evaluations of post-war prime ministers', *Political Quarterly* (2024).

CHAPTER 30

BY-ELECTIONS

Cowley's Law of By-Election Analysis is that too much attention is paid to who wins. Winning and losing is not a trivial part of the electoral process. It matters to the candidates; it matters to (some) constituents; and in a small number of cases, it may make a substantive difference to the government's majority.

But these are not the reasons by-elections attract the attention they do. The main reason we are interested in by-elections is because we see them as a measure – albeit an imperfect one – of a party's standing in the country. And at this point, the binary division between victory and defeat becomes much less important. If a party wins a constituency by five, fifty or 500 votes, the political lesson and significance should essentially be the same as if they lose it by five, fifty or 500. And yet it never is.

In 2021, for example, those around Keir Starmer were worried that they would face a leadership challenge if Labour lost the Batley and Spen by-election and that the Starmer project could be finished. Labour won by 323 votes. The idea that a party's leadership would be doomed if a party lost a seat by 300 votes but all is well if it wins by 300-ish is, by any objective standard, insane.

Or take the fallout from the Uxbridge by-election, a seat held by the Conservatives by just 495 votes in 2023. It was seen at the time as a glimmer of hope for the Tories, a victory gained because they had opposed the expansion of London's low-emission zone. Yet the lessons we learnt from that by-election should not have radically altered had 250 people voted differently.

Similarly, if the Conservatives had managed to narrowly hold Mid Bedfordshire or Tamworth, both lost by the party in 2023, the coverage would have been vastly different. But the lessons learnt – that the Conservatives were by then in the deepest of deep trouble – should have been exactly the same as if Labour had lost both seats by a small margin.

In part, this is because win/lose is such a simple and appealing metric. It makes for clear headlines. The party that wins will trumpet victory, even if that victory is by one vote. All of that is understandable and there is probably little that can be done about it. But once the initial excitement has subsided, harder-headed analysis should always focus on the swing, not on who won. By-elections are a noisy enough signal at the best of times. There is no need to make them even less useful by focusing on the wrong thing.

At this point, I could note that the late great David Butler, the founding father of British psephology, made a similar argument in print as long ago as 1949. Focus (with appropriate caution), he said, on the turnover in votes, not on the outcome. No one seems to have listened to him then, so they probably won't listen to me now.

Butler was writing at a time when by-elections were far more frequent than they are today. At their post-war peak, there were sixty-one between 1959 and 1964, far more than the twenty-three in the most recent parliament. Only six of the sixty-one saw a change in party control – although one of those was Orpington in 1962, an early sign of an increasingly volatile electorate.

Once that volatility led to by-elections becoming riskier, their numbers diminished. Fewer than half of those sixty-one between 1959 and 1964 were caused by the death of the sitting Member. The majority were caused by appointments to various external bodies or to the Lords, along with a handful of res-ignations. Once they knew that seats were more likely to change hands, party managers became less keen on these 'unforced' by-elections. While every four- or five-year parliament between 1945 and 1979 saw at least thirty by-elections, that has been true of only one parliament since 1979 – and that blip was caused by the mass resignation of Unionist MPs in 1985 as a protest against the Anglo-Irish Agreement.

But no government, however good its party management, can stop its MPs dying. The Grim Reaper therefore emerged as the most common cause of by-elections. As an interesting research paper recently published in the *Journal of Elections, Public*

Opinion and Parties noted, more than half of the by-elections since 1979 were caused by the death of Members.

Yet now things are changing again. The figure of twenty-three by-elections for the 2019 parliament is on the high side for recent years, more than in any parliament since 1992. And death has not been the main cause of by-elections since 2010. Of those twenty-three by-elections in the 2019 parliament, just five were the result of a Member's death.

One of the drivers of this is the Recall of MPs Act of 2015, which allows voters to recall an MP if they have been found guilty of misconduct. Many of the constitutional reforms proposed by the coalition government between 2010 and 2015 were stillborn – or have since been put down. But this one, criticised at the time for its timidity, has been much more consequential than many of its critics believed; I am happy to out myself here as someone who underestimated the impact it would have.

For recall to be triggered, it first requires the MP to have been found to have done something bad (mostly either a custodial prison sentence or suspension from the Commons for a non-trivial number of days); that then leads to a recall petition being opened, and if that is signed by 10 per cent of constituents, a by-election follows.

The number of by-elections caused directly by recall is still relatively small, but it is now just as common for MPs to resign because they know a recall petition is incoming. Take as an example the first by-election of the 2024 parliament. Mike

Amesbury's unique approach to MP–constituent relations – punching a voter repeatedly while on a night out – led to his conviction for common assault. Amesbury resigned his seat before the recall process could begin. Always better to jump than be pushed.

Further reading

D. Butler, 'Trends in British By-Elections', *Journal of Politics* (1949).

A. Middleton, 'Turnout, government performance and localism in contemporary by-elections', *Journal of Elections, Public Opinion and Parties* (2023).

CHAPTER 31

WHOOPS

Two decades ago, in his book on voter turnout, Mark Franklin argued that eighteen was about the worst possible age to first give people the vote. It's a transitional time in most lives, between school and the responsibilities of adulthood. Life at eighteen is full of distractions: some fun, some not, but all of which reduce the likelihood that anyone is going to prioritise going to a polling station. And since voting is habit-forming, this in turn has the effect of dampening participation in subsequent elections.

Franklin argued that lowering the voting age had been responsible for the widespread drop in turnout seen in many established democracies since the 1960s. It was therefore better for it to go back up or to go yet lower – and since he believed a return to a higher voting age was not politically feasible, he argued for lower.

Experience from Austria – which lowered the voting age to sixteen in 2007 – appeared to bear him out. A study published in 2019 analysed the effect of voting in the Austrian 2008 election, the first in which under-eighteens could vote, on later turnout in the 2013 contest. It detected a substantial effect. Comparing the behaviour of those who were able to vote for the first time in 2008 aged sixteen with those who just missed out in 2008 and who thus voted for the first time in 2013 aged twenty-one, it found turnout among the former by was higher by some 28 per cent.

At this point, I need to declare my interest. Ever since this idea was first floated, around the beginning of the century, I have argued against it. At one point, I even set up a website, now defunct, called Votes for Adults, to put the counter-case. I served on a thing called the Youth Citizenship Commission set up by Gordon Brown to examine the subject – along with some upstart president of the NUS called Wes Streeting. Whatever happened to him?

The policy produced the shortest media quote I've given in my career, when *The Sun* reported me as saying: 'It's a daft idea.'

I am not a fan. It's a daft idea.

Many of the arguments on first principles are flimsy at best or deceitful at worst. Marriage. Tax. Military service. Almost all of them are not really true or are just arbitrary.

Yet the Austrian experience seemed to offer a pragmatic, evidence-based benefit, one that should give even hardened opponents of franchise reform like me pause for thought. If it could raise turnout among young people by 28 per cent, maybe it was worth doing? The trouble is, it turns out it was cobblers.

Attempting to reanalyse the data, a new set of researchers

found they couldn't replicate the Austrian findings. Puzzled, they contacted the authors of the first paper – at which point, it became clear that an error in the original code had mangled the data on people's birth dates, rendering the whole analysis flawed.

With the correct data, the effect vanished. There was no longer any difference between those who voted for the first time in 2008 and those who just missed out. Attempts to identify any longer-term effects, by including the subsequent 2017 and 2019 elections in the new analysis, also proved null. There was basically no habituation effect.

If we wanted to be more precise about this, we would say that the researchers now couldn't find one. It's a golden rule of research that the absence of evidence of an effect isn't evidence of the absence of an effect. But still, where we once thought we had evidence of an effect, we now didn't.

This is all a bit embarrassing, although there are some silver linings if we look hard enough. For one thing, the new study did at least seem to show that lowering the voting age didn't make things worse. There was no evidence that reducing it led to lower participation in the future – although this is a long way from the claims frequently made for giving the vote to sixteen-year-olds by its advocates.

Perhaps more fundamentally, this was clearly a genuine mistake rather than the product of malice or fraud. And mistakes do happen. It's put well in John 8:7.

Alerted to their error, the original team did not try to bluster, bluff or double down; they fessed up. The first research paper now features a corrigendum notice, and a new paper, co-written with one of the original authors, has been published with the correct findings. The episode is a reminder to researchers to check their code carefully, but also, more generally, a reminder of the importance of replication studies and the need for people to make their data accessible, so that mistakes like this can be discovered.

We learn and we move on. Except, in this particular case, I wonder if we do. The claim about habituation has entered the political DNA. I've lost track of the number of times I've been told it happens – with Austria cited as evidence. Franklin's argument is plausible and we seemed to have evidence of it happening in a substantial way. The claim features, second hand, in all sorts of other publications. None of these, of course, have been withdrawn or feature the correction.

Plus, if the original paper gave me pause for thought, should the corrected one work the other way? Shouldn't discovering that there appears to be no habituation effect make advocates of lowering the voting age pause for thought? I bet it doesn't.

Further reading

M. Franklin, *Voter Turnout and the Dynamics of Electoral Competition in Established Democracies since 1945* (2004).

E. Graf et al., 'Revisiting eligibility effects of voting at 16: Insights from Austria based on regression discontinuity analyses', *Electoral Studies* (2024).

CHAPTER 32

INBETWEENERS

When Keir Mather won the Selby and Ainsty by-election for Labour in 2023, he was twenty-five – prompting discussion about whether he was too young for elected office. One government minister said he did not want Parliament to become 'a repeat of *The Inbetweeners*'. Sam Carling was just twenty-two when he won North West Cambridgeshire in 2024 – making him the first British parliamentarian to be born in the twenty-first century – attracting similar commentary.

They were curious debates, if that isn't too grand a word for them, given that there have always been a handful of youngish MPs and judgements about who is good enough to become an MP are traditionally made by a constituency's voters, not by commentators. I have an old-fashioned view on this: once the legal requirements are met, if the electorate think someone's old enough then they're old enough.

Yet for all that, there are some interesting issues involved in the representation of age. As fascinating research published in the journal *Government and Opposition* noted recently, young people are under-represented in almost every parliament in the world – and whereas recent decades have seen legislatures become more socially representative in other ways, there has been little, if any, improvement in the representation of youth.

You might be puzzled by this, because it may seem to you that MPs are getting younger, but I'm afraid that's just because you are getting older. The average age of the House of Commons has hovered at around fifty at every election in the past forty or so years, give or take a year. In 2024, it is sometimes said to have fallen to forty-eight, although this estimate is not based on a full sample – increasingly, MPs are refusing to divulge their dates of birth. Having dug around a bit, I think it is still nearer to forty-nine, not that it really matters much. What's a year between friends?

Either way, note that this figure is for the age of MPs elected at each general election. The average age then goes up every year until the subsequent election, so the actual average age of the Commons is always higher than the statistics you see anyway, by anything up to five years.

There have been some changes. Conservative MPs used to be younger on average than members of the Parliamentary Labour Party. In 1964, the average Conservative MP was a full seven years younger than the average Labour one; today, the average Labour MP is about three years younger than the average Tory.

There are also now fewer very old MPs; the introduction of

parliamentary pensions in the 1960s provided an alternative to clinging on to office for those without another income. Between 1945 and 1974, a full fifth of Labour MPs ended their parliamentary careers being carried out in a box. But essentially the House of Commons has long suffered from parliamentary middle-aged spread and any changes over the past few decades have been relatively minor.

The UK is not especially unusual in this. The Worldwide Age Representation in Parliaments (WARP) dataset – free to download and more fun than Wordle – contains data on the ages of the legislatures returned in over 800 elections across more than 180 countries. Some 57 per cent of these parliaments have an average age of between forty-seven and fifty-three. Turns out that parliamentary middle-aged spread is ubiquitous. Relative to their size in the population, MPs aged forty or less were underrepresented in 91 per cent of cases. For those aged thirty, the figure topped 99 per cent.

You might well object (and I'd agree with you, I think) that age isn't quite the same as some of the other representative characteristics that attract attention. It is, as the research paper noted, 'a temporary state of an individual's life'. One of the defining characteristics of young people is that they tend to grow up; when they do, they move from being part of an under-represented group to one that is over-represented. That is not true of most other under-represented groups. So maybe the under-representation of the young matters, but does it matter quite as much?

It is also not difficult to understand why some voters might be wary of young candidates and prefer those longer in the tooth. Other research found that when British voters were asked what sort of Parliament they wanted, they said they preferred one with more young MPs and fewer old ones. But that was in the aggregate. When offered a younger candidate as their MP, they tended to see them as less experienced.

Yet for all that, the problem here isn't really the electorate, because when given the choice of young candidates, they tend to be quite happy to vote for them as long as they are wearing the right colour rosette – as in Selby, where Mather achieved a 23.7 per cent swing, one of the largest in history, or in Cambridge-shire, where Carling overturned a Conservative majority of almost 26,000.

The problem, if it is one, is that parties don't stand all that many young candidates, almost certainly because party selec-torates tend to favour older candidates. At least up to a point, anyway. Because looking at the WARP data, I was struck by the fact that those aged sixty or over were also under-represented; that was true in over 70 per cent of cases. And although the data didn't break down the figures for those aged over seventy or eighty, you can bet this would be even worse.

Again, there are good reasons for this – and I am not sure we should want or expect too many octogenarian or nona-genarian parliamentarians. But it still often goes unnoticed and will become an even greater problem as populations age. At least parliamentarians were young once and they may vaguely remember what it was like; almost none of them have an understanding of what it is like to be very old. The article I mentioned earlier claimed to be on 'age inequalities in political representation', yet the under-representation of the elderly was not discussed, even once.

Further reading

D. Stockemer and A. Sundström, 'Introducing the Worldwide Age Representation in Parliaments (WARP) data set', *Social Science Quarterly* (2022).

D. Stockemer and A. Sundström, 'Age Inequalities in Political Representation', *Government and Opposition* (2023).

CHAPTER 33

REBELS

Faced with suboptimal polling during the previous parliament, some backbench Conservative MPs were said to be trying to dig in their constituencies – including by taking part in rebellions – to signal to their voters that they were different from the government. The logic went as follows: you may hate the Conservatives, but I am your local hard-working MP, who just happens to be a Conservative. I really am nothing to do with the government. Look, I've even voted against them! Vote for me!

To be fair, they were not the first MPs to think this – and they will not be the last. I'd give good money that in a few years you will find some Labour MPs desperately trying to signal their independence to their constituents. Keir Starmer? Never heard of him.

The modern MP's conjugation goes like this: *we* are unpopular; *they* are disliked; *she* is loathed; *he* is a publicity-seeking shyster; *I* am a popular local MP loved by my constituents.

Could it ever work? British elections remain largely party affairs, with the merits of the individual candidate being very much secondary – however much it appeals to the ego of some MPs to think otherwise. The 2019 British Election Study, for example, found just one in ten voters saying that their vote was based on the local candidate rather than national factors. Yet there is some evidence that MPs' personal vote has been growing in recent years, and estimates of the incumbency effect weigh in at around 2 percentage points for most Labour and Conservative MPs and higher still for those fighting their first election as an incumbent.

In a marginal seat, 2 percentage points is not to be sniffed at. Ditto for the one in ten voters who do vote for the local candidate. Working the parish pump hard therefore makes sense.

But how much do we think MPs' voting behaviour is going to matter in all of this? Here we can turn to two recently published bits of research, which reveal the answer to be, in short: not a lot.

On run-of-the-mill stuff, you might well not expect voters to notice how their MP voted, or even if they noticed, not to care very much. Voting in the House of Commons is transparent. Division lists are published online – whereas previously someone would have had to either subscribe to the parliamentary record or go to a library (like poor Dave in Chapter 23) – and harvested by multiple websites to allow voters to check the voting behaviour of MPs. Following high-profile rebellions, it is quite common for lists of MPs who have broken with their party to be published in the media. Still, while this information may be more accessible than in the past, most voters do not spend their time looking up the way their MPs have voted.

Yet the first of these two pieces of research looked at how MPs voted over Brexit – and that was about as good a test case as you could create. It was extremely high profile, on a polarising issue, with deep divisions within the parliamentary parties and plenty of cases where MPs were out of sync with their electorates. You would struggle to come up with a better test in a laboratory.

Even on Brexit, though, the electoral effects were extremely limited: just four MPs lost their seats in 2017 because of their position on the issue. The authors also surveyed MPs and found that their own estimates of the electoral sanction were just as limited as the reality. Not only were MPs not accountable for their voting but they knew they weren't.

Ah, you might say, sure, voters won't know about individual issues, but they will pick up on a more general impression of whether an MP is a loyalist or a free spirit, willing to kick against the pricks. But again, the answer seems to be no. Looking at every general election between 1997 and 2019, a second recently published piece of research (and here I must declare an interest as one of the authors) found no impact at all either. That was true whether you looked at aggregate election results or used surveys of voters to find if the ones with rebellious MPs behaved differently. It just didn't seem to matter whether MPs rebelled or not; it made next to no difference to their electoral fortunes.

You wouldn't expect to see large effects, anyway. If the total effect of the personal vote is 2 percentage points, an MP's voting is only ever going to be part of this. Yet what is surprising here isn't the small size of any effect but rather its almost complete absence.

This leaves us with a bit of a puzzle. There is plenty of evidence that MPs are increasingly willing to break ranks and defy their party managers. At the same time, British voters say they prefer MPs who demonstrate independence and who are willing to deviate from the party line. Yet they then don't reward them at the ballot box.

This is a useful reminder that we always need to be careful about polls that claim to tell us what voters say they want and in which people might well say one thing, only to then act differently. And it is a reminder that any MP thinking a bit of independence in the division lobbies is going to save them is likely to be disappointed.

MPs can rebel, or not, without many consequences. This isn't necessarily great news for democratic accountability. It's also bad news for anyone thinking that showing a bit of leg in the division lobbies will save them. 'We must all hang together, or most assuredly we will all hang separately,' as Benjamin Franklin probably didn't say.

Further reading

P. Cowley and R. Umit, 'Legislator Dissent Does Not Affect Electoral Outcomes', *British Journal of Political Science* (2022).

C. Hanretty et al., 'Members of Parliament are minimally accountable for their issue stances (and they know it)', *American Political Science Review* (2021).

CHAPTER 34

LOCKS

To misquote Sir Lewis Namier, party leadership elections are the locks on the canal of modern British history, regulating its flow. They are events at least as significant as general elections, but we know relatively little about them despite their importance.

Of all the British Prime Ministers since the end of the Second World War (excluding the incumbent, Keir Starmer, whose race is not yet run), only two, Attlee and Heath, both initially entered and finally exited Downing Street at a general election. The rest came in or left No. 10 mid-term. Of the past nine Prime Ministers (including Starmer), six came to power as a result of an internal party contest.

We know about the formal procedures involved. One of the guiding rules of British political journalism is that the processes parties use to choose their leaders must be described as complicated and arcane (bonus journalese points for 'Byzantine'), even when they are in fact relatively straightforward. We also have some enjoyable narrative descriptions of different contests, albeit of varying quality. Of Randolph Churchill's book *The Fight for the Tory Leadership*, an account of the events in 1963 that led to Alec Douglas-Home becoming Prime Minister, Iain Macleod wrote in *The Spectator* that four-fifths 'could have been compiled by anyone with a pair of scissors, a pot of paste and a built-in prejudice against Mr Butler'. Something similar could be said of many of the accounts of the contests since.

Yet our understanding of general elections has advanced so much in recent decades precisely because we have moved beyond an understanding of the formal rules and narrative accounts and tried – sometimes imperfectly, perhaps – to measure systematically what actually happened.

There have been some attempts to do this to leadership elections. Over thirty years ago, using aggregate data, Len Stark showed pretty convincingly that British leadership contests were driven by a hierarchy of needs: when choosing leaders, unity trumped electability and electability trumped policy preferences.

He also argued that the rules chosen didn't make much difference to the outcome. For all that parties obsessed about procedures, it was likely that the same people would have been elected in most cases, although the possible exceptions to this claim, including both Thatcher (in his sample) and Corbyn (since), strike me as important enough to treat that particular conclusion with some caution.

But there is a paradox here. Because when people have tried

to study the way MPs vote during leadership contests, a desire for unity and electability don't seem all that important; in study after study, the key divide seems to be more ideological.

Take, for example, the process by which Rishi Sunak reached No. 10. An excellent piece of research on the events of October 2022 finds clear differences between those who were known to have nominated Rishi Sunak, Boris Johnson or Penny Mordaunt. This was the latest in a line of studies tracking the way MPs have voted (or in this case, nominated) in leadership elections, and they all seem to show ideological divides are the key driver of the way MPs vote.

Sunak's support came disproportionately from socially liberal MPs who were, in the words of the authors, not as 'stridently pro-Brexit' as other parts of the parliamentary Conservative Party. Johnson, by contrast, attracted support from 'loyal hard-line Eurosceptics'. Other variables occasionally matter, but in different ways, this European divide was present in every Conservative leadership contest for which we have data between 1990 and 2019.

There are two issues with these sorts of studies, though, which I suspect will help explain this apparent paradox.

The first is perhaps obvious but relatively unimportant. Many of these contests, and all the ones that have changed Prime Minister, have involved secret ballots. While many MPs declare publicly who they are supporting, not all do – and we know some fib. We are therefore working with incomplete data. We know Boris

Johnson had at least 100 backers in late 2022; we know the identities of sixty-five of them. With a bit of detective work, we can usually patch together enough information to work out what's going on in broad terms, especially post hoc once we know how many votes each candidate received, but it's still a partial picture.

The second is less obvious but probably more significant. We don't know *why* MPs are voting that way. We can sometimes infer motives; if we find all the MPs of the right voting for a right-wing candidate and those on the left backing the left-wing candidate, we have a fairly good idea what's going on. But as always, it's the ones in the middle, the waverers and the floaters, where we need to know what's driving their vote. It would be plausible for the parliamentary swing voters to be the ones being driven by a desire for unity or electability, not ideology, and for them to be the ones making the difference in any contests.

To take one example, how do we test the importance of the (perceived) electability of the candidates? Usually, it is to see if MPs in marginal seats are more or less likely to back a certain candidate. This rarely shows any effect, but then perhaps we would be surprised if it did. Electability is a collective good as much as it is an individual one. MPs in all types of seats can be driven by a desire for an electorally successful candidate; those in marginal seats because they want to remain MPs, those in safer seats because they know that extended occupancy of the opposition benches is a miserable way to grind out your political career. Yet we have no way of detecting this. This isn't, by the way, a criticism of these authors – I've done the same sort of analysis plenty of times – it's more that we just lack the data to test it properly.

The same problems, with knobs on, apply if the wider membership is involved. What polling there is of the parties' grassroots has a good track record at telling us who is going to win. It is much less good at telling us *why*.

The perennial cry of the academic is that more research is needed. But when it comes to how we choose our Prime Ministers, it is justified. We need the equivalent of a British Election Study programme but for leadership contests. If anyone reading this wants to fund such a project, do get in touch.

Further reading

O. Booth et al., 'Selecting Sunak: Conservative MPs' Nomination Preferences in the (Second) British Conservative Party Leadership Election', *Parliamentary Affairs* (2023).

L. Stark, *Choosing a Leader: Party Leadership Contests in Britain from Macmillan to Blair* (1996).

CHAPTER 35

LOCALS

If you tried to design a system to predict how well political parties will do in a forthcoming general election, you would struggle to come up with anything much worse than British local government elections.

Different bits of the country go to the polls at different times, in different ways – a third of councillors in some places, half in others, in yet others everyone is up for election – and with differing electoral systems. There is low turnout and varying rates of candidature. And being local elections (the clue is in the name), plenty of local variation. Having spent election night as Radio 4's studio anorak for twenty years, I can assure you that few things annoy listeners more than when pundits treat the public's chance to vote for better local services as merely a proxy for a forthcoming general election.

Yet for all that, parochial factors – services, schools, scandals – can matter. Conservative councillors did not start losing seats in the mid-1990s in droves because they weren't paying enough attention to potholes; ditto for Labour in the run-up to 2010 or Lib Dems after 2010 ('Losing Here!'). There is always a national message being delivered too; it's just that sometimes it's difficult to tell exactly what it is.

It is best to ignore the raw numbers – councillors or councils gained and lost – because they are as dependent on what happened last time as they are on how well a party is doing this time. Parties can make gains, despite not polling especially well, as long as they do better than they did the last time those seats were fought. Equally, they can lose seats, despite polling relatively well, if it's less well than they did before.

To make matters even worse, results now trickle out over multiple days, especially when the local elections take place at the same time as other contests. Early results have a tendency to set a narrative that often proves flawed when the full picture becomes known and they allow parties to cherry-pick examples: 'Actually, I think it's been a mixed night for us; yes, we have lost badly in all of the bigger cities, but we're delighted to have gained a councillor in Market Snodsbury.' Although, occasionally a party will do so badly that they have little to spin. 'It's obviously a bad night for us, but things could have been worse...' – a statement that was true of the *Titanic*.

Ignore all that. Focus instead on the estimates of national performance. Confusingly, there are two of these (one produced by a team at the BBC, the other produced by Colin Rallings and Michael Thrasher), but while they often differ by a percentage point or two, they are never miles apart. We've had these estimates since the early 1980s and they enable sensible year-on-year comparisons.

But even these are projections of the *local* elections, an attempt to estimate what would have happened had there been contests across Britain. They are *not* forecasts of what will happen at a general election. Incumbent governments were behind in the local elections approaching 1992, 2001, 2005 and 2015, and yet still managed to achieve re-election. Even a double-digit lead for the Conservatives in 2004 was not sufficient to ensure victory the following year.

Local elections are what Karlheinz Reif and Hermann Schmitt termed 'second-order elections', used by voters to punish governing parties. Incumbents, therefore, often do worse. Despite this, a paper in *Electoral Studies* a few years ago showed that you could model general election results based on local election shares if you took into account both these mid-term blues and that the Lib Dems often do better in local elections compared to generals. Based on the 2013 and 2014 local elections, that model correctly predicted a Conservative victory at the subsequent general election, despite Labour being ahead in the locals.

Win big in the locals, though, and it can signify something more substantial. In the past forty years, there have only been three occasions when the incumbent government has been turfed out at a general election and replaced by the opposition – in 1997, 2010 and 2024. On all three occasions, the preceding local elections were a sign of what was to come. In the first two cases, the opposition party led by at least 15 percentage points. In 2024, while Labour's lead was less impressive, there was a miserable Conservative performance (the third worst for which we have data), along with a growing vote for the Lib Dems and the Greens.

For all that, I have a colleague who is puzzled by quite how obsessed the British political class are with local election results. What, he asks, do they tell us that opinion polls do not? It's a fair point. If you wanted to know if the Conservatives were in trouble in, say, 1996, you just needed to look at an opinion poll. Why bother with such detailed analysis of confusing second-order elections when we have polling that asks directly about people's intentions in the first-order election? It's akin to divining the weather forecast from the entrails of a chicken instead of using a meteorological satellite.

At least up to a point, that is. Given that polling does not have an unblemished record for accuracy, the local elections provide a check that they are in the right ballpark. They also provide a level of spatial detail that conventional opinion polls lack. Most opinion polls give a national picture. The geographic detail is always one of the benefits of actual elections. For MPs and for parties in particular, what local elections provide is a much more detailed understanding of exactly what is happening in their patch: which wards are solid, which are flaky. For those on the downslope, it's a sign of how bad things actually are. They provide proof that what they are seeing in the polls isn't something that is happening to other people; it's happening to them.

Further reading

C. Prosser, 'Do local elections predict the outcome of the next general election? Forecasting British general elections from local election national vote share estimates', *Electoral Studies* (2016).

K. Reif and H. Schmitt, 'Nine second-order national elections – a conceptual framework for the analysis of European election results', *European Journal of Political Research* (1980).

CHAPTER 36

FAKES

A few years ago, there was a research project that involved sending MPs emails from imaginary people. The fictious people came from different age groups and had names that suggested different ethnicities. The plan was to test if MPs were more likely to reply – or to reply in different ways – to people depending on who they were.

Similar work – what are known as correspondence studies – have been widely used to test discrimination in other areas of life. You send, say, otherwise identical CVs, save for details like the name or the age, and you test whether the white, or male or younger candidates were more likely to be invited to interview. It may not surprise you to discover that such studies do indeed often discover discrimination.

But when MPs discovered they were the ones being studied, there was uproar. The House of Commons Speaker Lindsay Hoyle criticised the academics involved, saying he was 'deeply concerned' about their conduct. He wrote to both the funding council and King's College London, where the study was based, and he said (and at this point things get a bit surreal) that he potentially viewed the research as a form of contempt of the House.

It wasn't pleasant seeing colleagues in the firing line – although given that I had long thought something like the study would be worth doing, there was also a sense of relief that my inability to get my arse into gear and get a project up and running had for once worked to my advantage.

Yet several things about the hoo-ha intrigued me. For one thing, there had been similar studies carried out in the past. A project published in 2019 with a very similar research design had ended up in one of the top academic journals in its field. It found that British MPs had a really high response rate to queries from their constituents, with 91 per cent responding (good news), albeit with some bias in their responses, depending on who it was they thought was writing to them (less good news).

Another similar project, published the same year, also found a very high response rate (89 per cent, with 70 per cent replying within a day), albeit again with some bias in the responses. Neither of these attracted any fuss or very much attention, and there are multiple similar studies published based on the responses of politicians in other countries.

The first difference between these studies was timing. This most recent experiment was conducted while MPs' offices were dealing with a huge increase in casework as a result of the pandemic. Their staff were under the Covid cosh – working from home, stressed, juggling home schooling and so on. Discovering that someone has chosen to increase your workload, however marginally, as part of an academic study must have smarted.

The project had been conceived and funded in a pre-Covid era and had already been delayed once after the pandemic broke out; it's difficult not to think that, in the circumstances, it might have been better had it been delayed again or even nixed entirely.

The second difference was that the university's ethics committee had insisted that the researchers carry out a debriefing after the experiment had taken place – and it was this that triggered the row. Had the researchers not been forced to write to MPs telling them that they had been part of a study, it's quite likely – probable, even – that none of them would have noticed. It's perhaps proof that transparency isn't always positive.

On its own, Hoyle's reprimand will be enough to deter most researchers dipping their toes into this particular research pool any time soon. No one wants to end up in leg irons. But at the risk of annoying MPs, I am not sure there is anything inherently wrong with the principle of the research. Or more precisely, if we accept this type of research method elsewhere (and any MP who has ever quoted one of those CV studies has implicitly done so), then it is difficult to see why politicians should somehow be considered out of bounds.

Indeed, I think you can go further. It is precisely because the work that MPs do in their constituencies is so important that it deserves proper study. The constituency face of the MP's role has become ever more important over the past few decades, with far greater engagement between MPs and their constituents than ever before. The days when an MP would swan into the constituency every couple of months, if that, and receive about a dozen letters a week are long gone. If it matters that people may be being discriminated against because of their sex or race when it comes to housing, it also matters if politicians do it, even if any bias is unconscious.

None of this is to argue that there are not ethical issues involved in work like this, whether it is MPs being surveyed or HR staff in some bank, and researchers have taken great pains to ensure that the enquires were simple and wouldn't take up too much of an MP's time. One concern must be that the fallout from this row makes ethics committees even more ultra-cautious than they already are (and boy, are some of them cautious). And as noted elsewhere in this volume, it can already be difficult to get British politicians involved with academic work and there must also be a risk that they will also become even harder to reach. All this would be very unfortunate. It would be a real shame if the timing of an otherwise justifiable study made research on Parliament harder to conduct.

MPs say that they take constituents' queries seriously, that partisan issues don't affect how they respond and that everyone gets a fair shake of the stick. The evidence from the existing research certainly shows that British parliamentarians respond much quicker than politicians in most other countries – so one of the many ironies of this row is that I suspect British MPs would have come out of the study really well. But now we'll never know.

A postscript: after writing the original column, other academics ran an experiment which asked voters if they were happy to have such studies run on their MPs. Short answer: yes.

Further reading

P. Habel and S. Birch, 'A Field Experiment on the Effects of Ethnicity and Socioeconomic Status on the Quality of Representation', *Legislative Studies Quarterly* (2019).

P. John et al., 'Using Citizen Voice to Evaluate Experiments on Politicians: A UK Survey Experiment', *Journal of Experimental Political Science* (2024).

CHAPTER 37

COCKROACHES

When the Conservative candidate was selected for the East-leigh by-election in 2013, the party's press release called her a 'local champion'. It said that she hoped to be the 'best local MP' the area had ever had; it described her as 'a mother of four who lives in the local area', claimed she knew what 'local people in the area care about' and said that the area needed 'a local MP we can trust'. In case anyone had missed the message, the party chairman added that she would be 'a brilliant local MP that people in Eastleigh can trust' and that she was 'already working hard for local people and is in tune with the community'.

They all do it. When the Liberal Democrats announced their candidate for the Tiverton and Honiton by-election in 2022, they described him as 'a local champion'. The press release noted where he lived, where he grew up and where in the constituency he volunteered; out of its twenty-five sentences, seventeen made some reference to his local roots.

During the 2024 general election, one candidate was criticised for not holding his birthday party within the boundaries of the constituency and another tried to demonstrate their local roots by noting that it was where they had lost their virginity.

I made up the last one, but the first is genuine and I do know of one Labour MP who talks about how he was conceived in his constituency, so it can only be a matter of time.

It all brings to mind the prediction made a few years ago by James Kirkup of the Social Market Foundation of a post-apocalyptic Britain 'in which all that will remain of life on earth will be cockroaches and Lib Dem activists handing out Focus leaflets attacking the cockroaches for not being local'.

It's easy to criticise. There isn't any evidence that MPs who have local roots are better than the ones that do not, and of all the subjects I've worked on, this is the one where there is the biggest gap between how practitioners and academics view things. Raise the importance of local roots with academics and they often shrug. Yet when I raise this with politicians, they look at me as if I am making a statement of the blindingly obvious. Politicians are acutely aware of how much voters care about this.

Dick Fenno, who almost fifty years ago wrote one of the best books about the links between members of the US Congress and their voters, had a theory about this. Academics, he argued, see it as a bit too parochial. He wrote:

Compared to a university, most congressional districts are less cosmopolitan. Members tend to be rooted in the values and the institutional life of local communities. They belong; they know where they belong; and it is the very strength of our representative institution that they do. The academic, on the other hand, is likely to be less locally rooted, more mobile, more attached to free-floating academic communities, an outsider in any context beyond the scholarly one.

Maybe. But regardless of the cause, in this particular clash between academics and politicians, the politicians are the ones who are right. Because when you ask voters, being local comes very high up their list of what they want from an MP.

It is all very well pointing out that Churchill, for example, did not have exactly deep roots in the constituencies he represented in Oldham, Manchester, Dundee or Epping. A similar complaint would apply to, say, Margaret Thatcher or Tony Blair. But people don't especially want to be represented by a Churchill, Thatcher or Blair. They want to be represented by someone they see as, well, representative. It's a collective-action problem: in the aggregate we might well want a Parliament bursting with talent and a decent number of statesmen or women, but that is not what voters want in their local MP.

Survey after survey finds that being local really matters to voters. One British study found it trumped all the demographic characteristics offered to respondents. Another study found that the distance between a voter's home and a candidate's home had an impact on their electoral performance.

Plus, for all that each election produces rows about parachuted candidates, the trend is actually in the opposite direction. A recent study published in the *Journal of Legislative Studies* finds that MPs are in fact becoming more local. Between 2010 and 2019, there was an election-on-election increase in the number who sat for constituencies, in the United Kingdom standard region, in which they were born. This applied to more than half of the House of Commons. Labour MPs were more local than Conservatives, but the increase was true across the board.

In some parts of the UK, being local is clearly very important. In Scotland and Northern Ireland, more than 90 per cent of MPs are local. In Wales, it is 75 per cent. In turn, MPs in the north of England (where the percentage varies from 56 per cent to 65 per cent) are more local than those from the south or the Midlands (all under 50 per cent), down to a mere 21 per cent in the east of England.

There are some obvious issues with using region (not least that regions are big), as well as place of birth (what if they grow up elsewhere?). But there are also some advantages, and anyway what matters more is the change over time. At every election since 2010, those entering the Commons have been more local than those exiting – and those coming in as a result of taking a seat have been more local than those who inherited a seat from the same party.

Although I have yet to see similar figures for the 2024 intake, it was very clear from the selection contests that having some form of link to the constituency was a key factor in determining who gets chosen to be a candidate, especially in many of the more winnable seats – so much so that some commentators have begun to worry that there is a danger this is all going too far. It's all getting a bit too *League of Gentleman*. Local MPs for local people; there's nothing for you here.

Further reading

P. Cowley et al., 'Increasingly local: the regional roots of British Members of Parliament, 2010–2019', *Journal of Legislative Studies* (2022).

R. Fenno, *Home Style: House Members in Their Districts* (1978).

CHAPTER 38

BOOTS

One of the biggest and yet often unremarked changes in British elections over the past twenty years has been the rise in postal voting. Before the turn of the century, fewer than 3 per cent of voters cast their ballot by post. Since the Representation of the People Act 2000 liberalised the rules, the numbers have increased dramatically and from 2015 onwards, postal votes have accounted for more than a fifth of those cast in general elections. In 2024, some 26 per cent of votes cast were by post. We no longer have polling day; we have polling *days*. Many voters cast their ballots weeks before the end of the campaign.

Given that anyone can get one now, those voting by post could be a perfectly representative sample of the population. Yet they are not. Some recently published research shows that four things seem to be especially important. Compare the over-75s to those aged eighteen to twenty-four and the former are over 20 percentage points more likely to be voting by post. Those with a disability that significantly limits their day-to-day activities are 13 percentage points more likely to vote by post than the non-disabled. (There is obviously some overlap between these two groups, but these figures are the independent effect on the likelihood of voting by post.)

The third important variable was constituency marginality, with voters in marginal seats more likely to opt for a postal vote. On the other hand, those with high levels of partisanship are *less* likely to vote by post – by a more modest 3 percentage points or so. Partisans still get a kick out of the expressive act of voting publicly.

In general, the findings all fit neatly with what is known as Downs's paradox of voting – which is, crudely put, that it is irrational to vote because the costs of voting (even when minimal) will be larger than the benefits multiplied by the probability of being the pivotal voter. This has been blowing the minds of first-year undergraduates ever since Anthony Downs first published his *An Economic Theory of Democracy* in the 1950s. They arrive at university with the belief that elections are crucial and voting is their civic duty, only to be told that they may as well not bother.

Despite Downs, voting remains the most common form of political participation. But where the costs of voting are higher, so is the likelihood of postal voting; ditto where there is more chance of being the pivotal voter. Plus, the real partisans are getting other expressive benefits out of the act of walking to a polling station. It's all pretty Downsian.

The other reason that postal-vote uptake will be higher in

marginal seats, however, is that parties campaign more in those seats – and those campaigns focus on signing up supporters for postal votes, because they are more likely to be returned (and because it then means there is less to do on polling day). In 2024, of the more than 9 million postal ballots issued, some 81 per cent were cast; that compares with polling station turnout of around 55 per cent.

For this sort of campaigning, political parties need boots on the ground – and for the most part, there are a lot fewer boots than there used to be, as party membership is in long-term decline. One of the most overused statistics in British politics is that the Royal Society for the Protection of Birds has more members than all the political parties put together. It's true, but it has always seemed a very unfair comparison. If you join the RSPB, they ask nothing more of you and they send you a magazine full of pictures of beautiful birds (and you used to get a free seed feeder). If you join the Labour Party, you get a magazine full of pictures of Keir Starmer and the chance to deliver leaflets on council estates in the rain. It is not really surprising that one is more popular than the other.

Political parties have long been made up of real enthusiasts, out fighting the good fight in all weathers, and those whose campaigning is mostly done from a sedentary position. It always comes as a surprise to some observers of politics – although, I have found, not usually to those in the parties themselves – to find out quite how many armchair party members there are, those who do very little or no campaigning. As another piece of recently published research showed, in the 2015 campaign, fewer than 45 per cent of Conservative or Labour members delivered any leaflets.

One of my Golden Rules of Political Life is that no one is ever allowed to criticise political parties or MPs for a lack of engagement with the public until they themselves have knocked on some doors and talked to some voters. When you've done that yourself, you can slag off those who do.

Increasingly, parties are supplementing members' activity with party supporters, those who are not members but who feel a very strong affiliation. This is what political scientists call the 'multi-speed membership party'.

Unsurprisingly, each individual supporter is less likely to campaign than any member, but there are just a lot more of the former. In 2015, for example, there were roughly forty times more people who said they felt very strongly Conservative than there were Conservative party members. This is a vast pool of labour for the parties, which, increasingly, is not going untapped.

Based on the figures in the research, you can, with some back-of-the-fag-packet calculations, work out that in 2015, both Labour and the Conservatives had more non-members delivering leaflets for them than they did members.

These sorts of estimates come with large potential errors, however. Plus, just because more supporters delivered leaflets doesn't mean that supporters delivered a larger quantity of leaflets. It could be that each member delivered multiple loads, whereas previously keen supporters did one batch, realised it was boring and went home to watch *EastEnders* instead. I know I would.

Further reading

J. Townsley et al., 'Who Votes by Post? Understanding the Drivers of Postal Voting in the 2019 British General Election', *Parliamentary Affairs* (2023).

P. Webb et al., 'So who really does the donkey work in multi-speed membership parties? Comparing the election campaign activity of party members and party supporters', *Electoral Studies* (2017).

CHAPTER 39

DISSENT

The party whips share one thing with Santa Claus: they both make lists of who's been naughty and who's been nice. These days, fewer MPs get presents.

I wrote the original version of this chapter in December 2023. The week before, the Sunak administration had suffered its first Commons defeat when twenty-two Conservative MPs backed an amendment on contaminated blood. It wasn't even the largest Conservative rebellion that night. About half an hour later, just under thirty voted against the government over the Draft Vehicle Emissions Trading Schemes Order. These two groups of rebels did not overlap much, a sign of how the government was getting it from both wings of the parliamentary party; that one night saw almost fifty Conservative MPs defy their whip and that's before we start to add in the many abstentions. A fortnight or so before, we'd had more than fifty Labour MPs vote against their whip over the party's stance on Gaza, including multiple frontbench resignations.

I did the final editing of this chapter in July 2025, on the same day Keir Starmer saw the largest rebellion of his government, when forty-nine Labour MPs voted against the second reading of the government's welfare reform bill. The rebellion would have been larger still had the government not announced significant concessions both the week before and during the debate; over 120 Labour MPs had signed a reasoned amendment against the bill and, less than a year after the election, a potential defeat had been on the horizon.

Whenever things like this happen, there is a lot of discussion of the individual circumstances. Is it the nature of the issue? Could it have been handled differently? Perhaps a new Chief Whip will turn things round? Spoiler: they never do, which is why there were seven Conservative Chief Whips between the 2015 and 2024 elections and yet backbench discipline remained poor.

While there are always short- or medium-term factors that help to explain any individual rebellion – the longer in office, the harder life gets for the whips, for example – there is also a much more fundamental truth behind much of what is going on: backbench dissent is now just a fact of parliamentary life.

MPs, of all parties and on all issues, have become increasingly willing to vote against their party line in recent years. As Philip (now Lord) Norton demonstrated convincingly decades ago, the period immediately after the Second World War saw extremely high levels of backbench cohesion, with only sporadic and mostly ineffective revolts. Between 1945 and 1970, there were no government defeats caused by government backbenchers rebelling in the House of Commons.

Those very occasional defeats that did take place occurred because of poor whipping or opposition ambushes (or both). Rates of rebellion by backbenchers were small or in some cases non-existent. There were two parliamentary sessions in the 1950s – that is, two whole years – when not a single government MP voted against the party line. The plot of C. P. Snow's 1964 novel *Corridors of Power* revolves around a minister who is brought down by backbench unrest – which consists of one MP voting against the party whip and a larger than expected number of abstentions. Those were the days.

Things began to change during the 1970s, and the past two decades in particular have seen record-breaking rebellion after record-breaking rebellion: over Iraq, university tuition fees, Lords reform and Europe. In 2005, I published a book pointing out that the parliament of 2001 was then the most rebellious in the post-war era. The parliament of 2005 then broke the record set by the parliament of 2001. And the parliament of 2010 in turn broke the record set by the parliament of 2005. Rebellion is in part learnt behaviour and today's MPs have had plenty of tuition.

Since 1970, almost every Prime Minister has been defeated as a result of their own MPs defying the whip. One exception is Liz Truss, but she holds this record in the same way that Sam Allardyce is the only unbeaten England football manager. Plus, she did her best not to be left out, as anyone who remembers the vote on fracking in October 2022 will recall. The government's victory there proved distinctly pyrrhic: the vote ended in chaos, with the Chief Whip threatening to resign and the PM announcing her own departure the very next day. If that's winning, you don't want to see losing.

The other exception is the current Prime Minister, Keir Starmer – at least so far, although things looked very dicey over welfare reform. Even Tony Blair found himself facing record levels of backbench dissent in his second term, winning some votes only narrowly; once his majority was reduced in 2005, he too was defeated in the Commons.

All this runs counter to much of the conventional wisdom about Parliament – which always sees the past as a golden age. The basic rule is that wherever you are in history, you will find people saying MPs in the past were more talented, brighter, smarter and braver. Back then (whenever *then* is), we had politicians of principle; now we have careerists. Then we had brave, independent MPs; now we have sheep. In R. B. McCallum and Alison Readman's *The British General Election of 1945* – the first in a series of books that continues to this day – it noted that there had been complaints about the diminishing quality of Members for 'the last fifteen years'. That is a House that contained Churchill, Attlee and Bevan.

Perhaps the most striking thing about the persistence of this belief in the myth of the independent backbencher of the past is not just that it's wrong but that it has been known to be wrong for so long.

When teaching this subject to students, I always try to get the balance right between noting the rise in backbench independence and yet at the same time impressing upon them that party still dominates in the Commons. Most votes still see complete cohesion; most rebellions are small and ineffectual. Most MPs rebel extremely rarely in absolute terms, even if more than they used to. The influence of the whips remains greatest on run-of-the-mill votes, on issues few know or care much about and where MPs are happy to be guided.

Decades ago, Jeremy Corbyn made a similar point to his whip, saying that for all his rebellions, he mostly voted the party line. Yes, his whip replied, but not when it mattered.

Further reading

P. Cowley, *The Rebels* (2005).

P. Norton, *Dissension in the House of Commons 1945–1974* (1975).

CHAPTER 40

PREDICTIONS

Shortly after Labour lost three consecutive elections in the 1950s came the publication of *Must Labour Lose?* The book's authors were savvy enough to include the question mark in the title, but that didn't mask the fact that the book was essentially all about Labour's electoral woes. It detailed multiple challenges the party faced as British society changed and its ties with the working-class diminished.

Yet it turned out Labour didn't have to lose. It was the Conservatives who were defeated in four of the following five general elections.

Decades later, after Labour suffered its fourth consecutive general election defeat in 1992, there were a series of articles and books arguing that Britain had become a de facto one-party state with perpetual Conservative rule. The British Election Study that year was entitled *Labour's Last Chance?* Again, note the question mark, but it too was not an optimistic book for any Labour supporters.

Yet within months came exit from the Exchange Rate Mechanism, an event from which John Major's Conservative government never recovered. The next election inaugurated Labour's most electorally dominant period since its formation.

More recently, it was the Conservative Party that was variously said to be doomed. You may have read books with titles like Geoffrey Wheatcroft's *The Strange Death of Tory England* (published without the saving grace of a question mark), which came out in early 2005 just before the Conservatives crashed to their third consecutive defeat. When David Cameron became party leader, the Conservatives held under 200 seats. Yet five years later, he was in No. 10.

Perhaps you remember the discussion from a decade or so ago about how it was now next to impossible for British political parties to win majorities anymore. Everything was about how minority governments had become the new normal and we all had to get used to coalitions. Then 2015, 2019 and 2024 all produced majority governments, the last a landslide of Blairite proportions.

Or maybe you can't remember any of that, but your memory is just about good enough to recall the discussion following the 2019 election. Labour was finished. They'd lost Scotland for good. Brexit had created an irreversible split between Labour and many of its northern constituencies.

This, to be fair, wasn't just external observers or commentators. It was noticeable during the Labour leadership election of 2019 how relatively few of the endorsements of the various candidates for the party leadership bothered to mention how good they would be as Prime Minister. It was all about how they could rebuild the party or engage with the public. It was widely assumed this was, at best, a two-term project.

And yet here we are.

Lest anyone think I'm being uncharitable to any of my colleagues and their work, I am happy to admit that the only reason I have not included any of my own erroneous predictions is because there would be too many of them to list. 'Prediction is very difficult,' the Danish physicist Niels Bohr is said to have remarked, 'especially about the future.'

It is indeed, and we need to be a bit more cautious about our powers of prediction when it comes to the fate of political parties.

Wheatcroft's book title was a nod to George Dangerfield's book *The Strange Death of Liberal England*, which detailed how the Liberal Party went so rapidly from its landslide victory in 1906 to the margins of politics. 'From that victory they never recovered,' he wrote. It's still widely read, if much criticised by historians, but it came out in 1935. It was a work of history, not prediction.

The past few years have shown both the dangers of writing off parties and that the apparent hegemony of any political party is always largely illusory. In Scotland, in just fourteen years, the SNP went from six MPs in 2010 to almost total dominance and then back down to nine MPs in 2024. At one point, in the darkest days of the 2017 election, the Liberal Democrats' internal polling had them on course to win just one seat. The head of their campaign found himself thinking that he might well be the last person ever to hold that role. It wasn't at all obvious that party would survive. Seven years later, Ed Davey found himself with the largest number of Lib Dem MPs ever and the largest for any of their predecessor parties for a century.

We are in an era where Labour can lose Sedgefield, Tony Blair's old seat, in 2019, and the Conservatives can lose Witney, Maidenhead, Uxbridge & South Ruislip and South West Norfolk – the seats of Cameron, May, Johnson and Truss respectively – in 2024. Who knows where we will be in 2028 or 2029?

Even sixty years on, *Must Labour Lose?* remains a fascinating read, albeit now very much of its time. Since then, the quality of research and the data on which it is based have all got much better. But these studies are often very good at telling you what happened and why. They are much less good at telling you what is to come.

Further reading

M. Abrams and R. Rose, *Must Labour Lose?* (1960).

A. Heath et al., *Labour's Last Chance?* (1994).

CHAPTER 41

LETTERS

A new MP soon discovers that their postbag is an imperfect measure of public opinion. They quickly learn to filter out the coordinated letter-writing or email campaigns. They learn to ignore the correspondent who claims they will never vote for them again but who has made this threat at least a dozen times before and who never voted for them in the first place anyway.

The sorts of issues that can provoke people into writing – or get them steamed up on social media – are not necessarily those that matter much to most of their constituents. As one MP told me a long time ago: 'God writes an awful lot of letters.' The same applies to those who like foxes.

But equally, when something does cut through and properly riles people, MPs learn to take note. This is why in 2020 I found myself thinking about the poll tax, almost a quarter of a century after it was abolished.

The first academic article I ever wrote, what feels like a life-time ago, examined the pressure Conservative MPs faced from their constituents over the poll tax in the late 1980s – and one feature of that was that they got a lot of post.

Many MPs said it was the most correspondence they'd ever had on any issue. It was variously described to me as 'enormous', 'tremendous', the 'biggest amount I can ever remember', 'a mass, an absolute mass', 'a colossal amount, certainly the biggest amount of correspondence I've ever had', 'absolutely ginormous', 'enormous' and 'it dwarfed anything I got on any other single issue', leaving MPs 'inundated'.

Yet what really marked out the poll-tax post was not just its scale but its nature. The letters tended to come from individuals, by and large not coordinated by outside groups. These, said one MP, 'were people writing in their own hand on a quality of notepaper which ranged from Basildon Bond down to the lined paper picked up in a supermarket'.

Then there was the nature of those writing, who were not just the usual suspects. The letters were also specific; most went beyond 'I don't like this' and instead set out why they didn't like it, often in detail and based on the way the policy was affecting them. There was also a near-constant level of correspondence on the poll tax, which is very different to the correspondence MPs received on some other issues, with the letters coming in a flood but then dying away quickly. And last, there was no countervailing pressure: few constituents wrote in support of the poll tax.

The reason I found myself thinking about it in 2020 was because Dominic Cummings had gone for a drive to Barnard

Castle. This is one of those political references which almost everyone reading this book will understand but will be difficult to explain in the future. Imagine being a history teacher in fifty years' time. 'Sir, sir… I don't understand, sir. He drove in his car to test his eyesight?' 'Yes, class, he did.' It'll make teachers fondly reminisce for the easy days when they had to teach the Schleswig–Holstein question.

As today's reader knows, Mr Cummings's travel itinerary wasn't tremendously popular when it became public knowledge in 2020 and MPs claimed to be getting a lot of correspondence on it from their constituents, much of which sounded, to me, almost identical to that received over the poll tax.

One word of warning here: you should always treat MPs' claims about their postbags with some scepticism. It turns out they may not always be telling the truth. One MP once told me that you should never claim to have received no letters on something, because that could be disproved, but beyond that, anything went. You should be especially careful about claims from opposition MPs, who in a case like this one had an incentive to accentuate the negative.

But enough Conservative MPs, privately or publicly, were admitting to receiving a flood of correspondence over the Cummings affair – even many of his supporters. Danny Kruger, then the MP for Devizes, who had been strongly supportive of Dominic Cummings, admitted that his inbox had been 'horrific'.

And the nature of the inboxes sounded remarkably similar to

back in 1990: largely uncoordinated, personal, detailed (in the Tory MP Mark Pawsey's words: 'sometimes in heartbreaking detail'), not from the usual suspects and mostly one-sided.

Things are different now, of course. Back then it would have been letters, but there's much less Basildon Bond these days: the 4.7 million pieces of post arriving at Westminster in 2005 had fallen to just over 1.2 million by 2019 and is now below the million mark every year. Email has grown to replace it, which just makes the process faster and more immediate. But the rest all seems very similar.

This isn't to put Mr Cummings's excursion on a par with the poll tax – although as a wider public policy issue, Covid was clearly more significant than the poll tax, both at a micro and a macro level. It's merely to say that the sort of feedback MPs were getting over this sounds remarkably similar and of the sort to make MPs sit up and take notice.

MPs should also note that the nature of the reply matters. In a different study, in 2013, Rosie Campbell and I asked people how satisfied they were with their MP. On average, those who had been in touch with their MP were more positive than those who had not. But a lot depended on the nature of the interaction. Of those who had contacted their MP and said they were 'very satisfied' with the response, 86 per cent said that they were satisfied with the MP and just 3 per cent were not, a net score of +83. At the other end of the scale, of those who had contacted their MP and were 'very dissatisfied' with the response, the score was -93, which is about as bad as you can get.

Further reading

P. Cowley, 'Parliament and the poll tax: A case study in parliamentary pressure', *Journal of Legislative Studies* (1995).

CURVILINEAR

You have probably not heard of May's Law of Curvilinear Disparity, although your view of party politics may well be similar to it.

It's named after the political scientist John May, who in 1973 argued that those lowest and highest in a political party's hierarchy were the least likely to hold 'extreme' views, while those in the middle of parties, the party activists, were the most likely to have views further away from the average voter.

If you try to plot the various positions of voters, members and leadership on a graph, you get a curve. Do it for a second party and you get another curve, in the opposite direction. Collectively, they resemble a pair of parentheses, like so: ( ). Close to each other at the top and bottom, they are further away in the middle. Hence, curvilinear disparity.

May's Law gets praised for its simplicity and it accords with much of the common wisdom on political parties. The idea of the radical activist, out of touch with the voters, is a common one that you hear all the time in political conversations.

Yet for all that people make these sorts of claims, it is much less common to see them tested. May's original 1973 article lacked any systematic evidence to support his law – he said it had an 'aura of verisimilitude' based on 'respectable testimony and some harder evidence'. That's the sort of thing you could get away with in the 1970s.

The obvious problem is that to test it properly you need some way of simultaneously measuring the beliefs of three groups of people in two parties. One way could be surveys, in which the same questions were posed at roughly the same time to voters, members and MPs – but this isn't easy or cheap, which explains why it is so rarely done.

The good news is that there was just such a systematic test of May's Law recently. And it showed not only that May's Law doesn't seem to hold any more – if indeed, it ever did – but also that both of the main political parties were seriously out of touch with their own electorates.

The researchers used two batches of questions commonly employed by social scientists to measure people's economic and social values. These were designed to tap into underlying, stable, long-term ideological attitudes, rather than ephemeral, short-term policy preferences. Five questions cover economic values, for example: should government redistribute income from those who are better off to those who are less well off? Five others measure what are often known as liberal-authoritarian attitudes. Another example: do young people have enough respect for traditional British values?

Combine these questions into scales and you see exactly the sort of thing May predicted – or at least you do with the Labour Party and economic values. Labour's members were indeed more radical on the economy than both Labour MPs and Labour voters.

These differences were not massive, though, and there was almost no difference between the different types of members depending on their levels of activism. This is another of the things frequently claimed about political parties – that the armchair members are moderate, those prepared to pound the street are loopy – and yet there was relatively little evidence of it.

Perhaps more importantly, this was the only time May's Law was valid. It did not hold when the researchers examined the Conservative Party's relationship with economic values. Rather than being closer to the average voter, Conservative MPs actually sat to the right of Tory members. In turn, the rest of the party sat some distance to the right of their voters. There was a clear gap between the views of Conservative voters and the Conservative parliamentary party and an even bigger gap between Tory MPs and the average voter. On four out of the five questions asked about economic matters in the surveys, those who backed the

Conservative Party at the polls had more in common with the Labour Party than they did with Conservative members, activists and MPs.

In other words, the Conservatives were less), more /. Overall then, on the economy, instead of ( ), we had something like (/.

On social values, you saw something completely different again – with both parties' MPs sitting to the left of their wider party, who were in turn to the left of their voters. The effect of this was that the average British adult was more socially conservative than the average Conservative MP. Indeed, on these issues, Conservative MPs had views that more closely aligned with the average Labour voter than they did with their own supporters. Not), but \.

For Labour, there was also serious disconnect between their voters and the party, and even more so between the party and the average voter. Just to give one example, that there should be tougher sentences for those who break the law was the view of 24 per cent of Labour MPs and 25 per cent of members, but it was backed by 53 per cent of those who voted Labour in 2019 and 70 per cent of the public at large. Again, \ rather than (.

In other words, on social matters overall, rather than ( ), we had \ \.

Ideally, those voting for a party would broadly share its basic values; its representatives would in turn share the values of the party membership. Neither major British party could claim this. Labour were relatively close to their voters on economic issues but way out of kilter on social issues. For the Conservatives, the opposite was the case.

What we don't know is whether this is a new (and worrying) development or whether it has always been true. We don't know, and will never know, whether May's Law used to hold but recent changes to the party system or the electorate mean it no longer does. Or maybe it was never true in the first place.

Further reading

J. May, 'Opinion Structure of Political Parties: The Special Law of Curvilinear Disparity', *Political Studies* (1973).

A. Wager et al., 'The Death of May's Law: Intra- and Inter-Party Value Differences in Britain's Labour and Conservative Parties', *Political Studies* (2022).

CHAPTER 43

ISHOOS

'**B**low for Starmer as poll finds majority of public oppose lowering the voting age to sixteen – in damning verdict on Labour's flagship policy.'

That was the headline in the *Daily Mail* at one point during the 2024 general election campaign, reporting a new poll which found that 52 per cent of the public were opposed to lowering the voting age, compared to 38 per cent who supported the policy.

Let's leave aside that the poll also showed Labour leading the Conservatives by 24 percentage points – many more blows as bad as that one and Labour might just go on to win a landslide. Let's leave aside that it was a bit of a stretch to describe votes at sixteen as Labour's flagship policy; the text of the article later described it as *one of* Labour's flagship policies, although even that was pushing it a bit. Let's leave aside that the same poll found that 50 per cent opposed the Conservative government's much more high-profile proposals for national service. In fact, let's excuse all of this as a partisan headline writer's hyperbole and move on.

Let's focus instead just on the fact that the majority of the public opposed lowering the voting age. This is long-established Labour policy, a policy which Keir Starmer reaffirmed his commitment to during the election campaign (and to which his government then reaffirmed its support in mid-2025).

So, could it matter that a majority of the population opposed it? Flagship or not, could something like this hurt Labour?

As noted elsewhere in this volume, I yield to no one in my scepticism about the wisdom of lowering the voting age. Yet this poll wasn't especially a blow to the Labour Party. It wasn't a surprise. There were almost no reasons to think that it would hurt Labour at the election – and since polling day, no evidence has shown that it did.

For one thing, it came as no surprise to discover that there was majority opposition to the policy, because most surveys have shown this for decades. Votes at sixteen has long been a niche interest. Indeed, several years ago, the Hansard Society carried out a survey that asked respondents which aspects of the constitution they understood and which they approved of. The only one to have both majority understanding and approval was voting at eighteen – and it has long seemed to me curious that we would change the only bit of the constitution that people understood and liked.

But to understand the scepticism that this was bad news for

Labour, you need to think about how people vote – and especially about the way the electorate deal with what Tony Benn used to call 'the ishoos'. More than half a century ago, the great political science pairing of David Butler and Donald Stokes, in their groundbreaking book *Political Change in Britain*, noted that four conditions needed to be met to determine how a voter behaved in the polling station in response to a political issue.

First, the voter needed to be aware of an issue. Second, they needed to have an attitude or opinion on it. Third, the parties needed to have differing stances on the issue. And then fourth, the voter needed to vote for the party with the stance that was closest to theirs.

These are quite high bars and many issues fail to clear them. You would be surprised – or perhaps you wouldn't be? – by how many don't even clear the first two hurdles. Things that can obsess politicians or journalists pass many voters by entirely. One of my favourite electoral statistics is that in 1964, some 40 per cent of respondents to the British Election Study could not name two political issues facing the country. Note that they did not have to do anything especially sophisticated with this information, such as saying what they thought about the issues or what they believed the party's stances on the issues to be. They just had to *name* two issues, and yet even that was beyond four in ten of the population.

True, 1964 was a long time ago. As voters have become less stable in their political support with lower partisan alignment, as psephologists put it, so issue voting has become more important, but still relatively few issues clear all four of these hurdles. Even when the public know about an issue, they often don't have a view on it, or the parties don't differ that much (or if they do, the public don't see the differences) – and even if they do, voters don't then vote accordingly.

In the case of the poll reported by the *Daily Mail*, many voters will have been entirely unaware that there were arguments over franchise reform. That 90 per cent had a view when asked by a pollster is not quite the same as 90 per cent of people having given it the slightest thought as they went about their normal life. There were, at least, differences between the parties on the policy (although again, without prompting, how many voters knew those differences?), but it seems unlikely that even to voters who did know, it would be the sort of issue that would matter enough to actually make someone vote one way or another.

Even I didn't let it determine my choice of vote – and it's difficult to think of who might. For some people, issues like this provide a convenient excuse or justification. ('I was thinking about voting Labour, but then I heard they wanted votes at sixteen,' says someone who has voted Conservative all their life...)

And for Labour, the policy had obvious advantages. Once implemented, the new voters it enfranchises are more likely not to be Conservative-supporting (at least in the short term). Labour politicians will deny that this is why they are doing it – short-term partisan reasoning driving constitutional reform!

Whatever next? But the electoral benefit of this will be small, if it exists at all; just because the newly enfranchised voters are likely not to be Conservative does not, I suspect, mean they will necessarily be Labour-supporting either.

You might well think that things like this would be better done on a cross-party basis. But Labour politicians were able to respond easily enough by pivoting to areas on which the Conservatives have acted in a way that lacked cross-party agreement. ('I will take no lectures about partisanship from the people who introduced a system of voter ID designed to lower turnout and keep young people away from the polls.')

And whatever its merits, votes at sixteen did at least have the vague whiff of being a policy, maybe even a moderately radical one. It also doesn't cost much. Giving young people the vote is a lot cheaper than giving them houses.

Further reading

D. Butler and D. Stokes, *Political Change in Britain* (1969).

CHAPTER 44

SPLITS

Whenever there is a high-profile free vote in Parliament – one where the party whips do not issue instructions to MPs on how to vote – you will see frequent claims that it cuts across party lines, that the issues involved are 'non-party', 'cross-party' or 'not issues of party politics'. There is some truth in this, although it also reflects an anti-party sentiment that has long existed. Writing at the beginning of the twentieth century, Sidney Low noted that the easiest way to get a round of applause at a public meeting was to claim that something was non-partisan. 'No sentiment', he said, 'is likely to elicit more applause at a public meeting, than the sentiment that "this, Mr Chairman, is not a party question, and I do not propose to treat it from a party standpoint".' Not a lot has changed since, except that we now have fewer public meetings.

That these sorts of issues – sometimes referred to as issues of conscience – split the parties is obvious. This is in large part *why* they are free votes. It is a lot easier to allow MPs to vote as they like rather than trying to impose a whip. Free votes are often more an acceptance of reality than some grand constitutional principle.

When they come before Parliament, issues of conscience tend to be supported and opposed by a range of MPs on both sides of the House and advocates often go out of their way to stress the cross-party nature of their support. This is unusual given that most normal votes see complete party cohesion, with no MPs voting against their party line. As a result, the issues are usually reported differently in the media. Precisely because they are not the norm, the free vote and the extent of cross-party support are highlighted and the focus of reporting is not (as it usually is) the split between government and opposition.

But by doing so, the media and politicians are concentrating on the exceptions (that is, MPs voting against the majority of their party) and often overlook the norm (which is that most MPs are not doing so). Perhaps the worst example of this I have seen was when two Labour MPs voted against banning fox hunting in 1997 and eight Conservative MPs voted in favour of a ban. This was reported by *The Times* as saying they 'had defied conventional wisdom about the politics of hunting'. Yet 374 Labour MPs (99 per cent of those voting) had supported a ban and 128 Conservatives (94 per cent) had opposed it. The conventional wisdom was pretty on the mark.

There are two useful rules with these types of votes. The first is that usually, even with the whips off, the majority of Labour MPs will go in one lobby and will face the majority of Conservative MPs in the other. The second is that while these issues split some of the parties some of the time, they rarely split all the parties all of the time.

The vote on assisted dying in late 2024 is a good example. All the larger parties split, as did some of the smaller parties. But the divisions were not equal.

To find out the extent of the divisions, we can use a measure called the Index of Party Unity. It's pretty basic: you subtract the minority percentage of a party's voting MPs away from the majority and divide by 100. A united party scores 1.00. One that has split right down the middle scores 0.00.

At the bill's second reading vote, Reform and Labour split the worst, with roughly 60/40 splits, producing scores of 0.20 and 0.23 respectively. (I have included tellers in all calculations.) These are relatively deep splits, but they are not record-breakers. There have been multiple occasions on which parties have divided worse than this in the past. Without breaking sweat, I can show you deeper splits than 0.20 among the major parties in the past few decades on a range of issues, from capital punishment to divorce, from the compulsory wearing of seatbelts to the age of consent and from obscene publications to embryo and stem cell research.

On assisted dying, the majority of the Lib Dems (0.69), Plaid (0.50) and all the Greens (1.0) also voted in favour, as did one independent MP and one SDLP MP.

Facing them in the no lobby, however, were the majority of Conservative MPs (an 80/20 split, so a score of 0.60), along with most of the independents who voted and the majority of the MPs from Northern Ireland, with the DUP's 1.0 score mirroring the Greens. The SNP abstained en masse.

In other words, of the parties with more than two MPs voting, the issue split two quite badly, caused some division among three and saw unity among two – and saw most Labour MPs facing most Conservative MPs.

Critics of Parliament love free votes, love the idea of the normally chained MP set free from the evil whip in some temporary act of liberation, like so many heirs of Spartacus (to borrow a phrase from an essay by Peter Jones on the subject). Yet even freed from the constraints of the party whip and even on hot-button issues like this one, most MPs still end up voting with members of the same party. Even on free votes, the party label is almost always the single best indicator of how someone will be voting.

Free votes are a useful reminder that the voting cohesion we see at Westminster or elsewhere is not entirely artificial or imposed; at root, it reflects genuine differences in values and viewpoints.

And the consequence of this is that for all we talk about them being non-party, and even with the whips off, the outcome of free votes is largely dependent on the partisan composition of the House. Holding everything else constant, had there been 100 fewer Labour MPs and 100 more Conservatives taking part, the bill to legalise assisted dying would have fallen at second reading by a majority of one.

Further reading

P. Cowley and M. Stuart, 'Sodomy, Slaughter, Sunday Shopping and Seatbelts: Free Votes in the House of Commons, 1979 to 1996', *Party Politics* (1997).

P. Jones, 'Members of Parliament and Issues of Conscience', in his *Party, Parliament and Personality* (1995).

CHAPTER 45

N

How many times has a British governing party recovered electorally from being consistently 15–20 percentage points behind in the polls? On my reading of the data the answer is zero, although it does partly depend on how you define 'consistently'.

But also, how many times has a government *been* consistently 15–20 percentage points behind in the polls? Again, there are some definitional issues, but I think we can make a case for three occasions, all involving Conservative premiers: before 1945 (albeit with relatively limited polling), 1997 and 2024.

In all three cases, the actual election result involved a smaller gap in votes than the polls had predicted, although still sizeable in each case and all led to Labour landslides.

So, when a party is consistently 15–20 points behind, can we declare Game Over? Well, maybe. It's clearly not a good place to be. But we have here a success rate for the Conservatives of 0 per cent, out of just three cases. How wise do we think it is to make predictions about *future* behaviour based on just three cases – or what my data-minded colleagues would call an N (for number of cases) of three?

This is all part of a wider problem, which I discuss in my yet-to-be written magnum opus *The Small N Problem in Electoral Studies* (Wishful Thinking Publications, 2028). Put simply, we just don't have enough elections.

There have been twenty-nine general elections in Britain since women and working-class men gained the vote in 1918 and twenty-five since equal suffrage ten years later. There have been just twenty-one since one-person, one-vote became universal in 1950.

Even if all twenty-one had been fought under similar conditions, this would still be a small sample on which to base predictions. And we know, of course, that they have not been fought under similar conditions. Instead, there have been dramatic changes in things like the party system, campaigning techniques, the media, and voter demographics and behaviour, all of which narrows our sensible frame of reference yet further. We can make relatively few predictions about modern-day election campaigns based on our knowledge of what happened in, say, 1955.

One reason why the number of elections where a party was 15–20 points behind in the polls is so limited is because polling is relatively recent. We don't know, for example, if Balfour was behind by 15 points in the run-up to 1906. We have polling from the 1940s onwards, but it is patchy initially; we only have good panel surveys since the establishment of the British Election Study in 1964. Sixty years sounds like a long time, but that is only seventeen elections – and the one thing the British Election Study shows more perhaps than anything else is how voter behaviour has been changing over time.

Take, for example, the rise of voter volatility, as detailed in the most recent book from the British Election Study team. There is a famous quote attributed to Harold Macmillan ('Events, dear boy, events') about the power of circumstances to derail even the best-laid plans. Just because it would appear to be entirely apocryphal does not undermine its value. One consequence of voters being less solidly aligned with parties is that events can now move voters in a way they might not have previously.

How many election campaigns have seen sizeable shifts in the levels of party support? Again, it partly depends how you define sizeable, but I think the answer is just two: 2010, when the Lib Dems surged, only to then deflate before polling day itself, and 2017, when Labour went from 20+ percentage points behind to denying Theresa May a majority. Should we see that as just two out of the twenty-one elections since 1950 – in other words, as infrequent events that are probably unlikely? Or we should see them as two out of the past five, yet another sign of how much more volatile voters are becoming?

You might similarly note that the opinion polls seen in the 2024 parliament ranged from a Conservative lead of 26 points to a Labour lead of 39, a larger spread than in any post-war parliament. And as some new research on the 2024 election makes clear, they also mark the highest volatility in actual votes for decades. The Pedersen index, which measures changes in the aggregate vote shares of parties between elections, was higher in 2024 than at any time since the 1931 election, while the individual volatility of voters, the extent to which they change between elections, was the highest for which we have data. What the electorate giveth, it can take away.

And then think about the specific circumstances of different contests. How many elections were fought, as the 2024 one was, after the incumbent party had been in office for more than a decade? Since 1945: just five. How many of those were fought by a different PM to the one who won the previous election? The answer is four, of which one resulted in a government victory. How many were fought by a different PM to the one who took over from the one who fought the previous election? Just one.

In the run-up to 2024, we kept reading pieces on whether the election would end up like 1992 or 1997, because the number of cases that it could resemble was just so limited. It ended up not being like either, really. More like 1997 than 1992, maybe, but not really that much like 1997 either. The 2024 election was like, well, the 2024 election.

Further reading

E. Fieldhouse et al., *Electoral Shocks: The Volatile Voter in a Turbulent World* (2020).

C. Prosser, 'Fragmentation revisited: The UK General Election of 2024', *West European Politics* (2024).

CHAPTER 46

BATS

Do you remember the 'Vote Labour and the bats get it' part of the election campaign? I must have missed it; maybe I just wasn't paying enough attention. Which is curious, because bats are a big deal at Cowley Towers and had I clocked Labour's chiroptophobic tendencies, I would have abandoned all academic neutrality and been out on the doorstep, day and night, urging the electorate to get Keir Starmer into No. 10 sharpish.

Much of the current discussion around relaxing planning regulations has focused on the effect on large-scale developers and big-ticket projects like HS2. But having just done a domestic renovation, I know how these same rules can affect run-of-the-mill properties as well – and just how ruinously expensive they can be.

Raising the subject produces three very distinct reactions from people. From those who've heard it before, a look that says *Oh no, here he goes again, I preferred it when he was talking about politics*. From those hearing it for the first time, there is instead puzzlement or disbelief. *This can't be right*, you can see them thinking. *He must be confused or exaggerating for comic effect; if I nod a lot, he'll stop soon.* But then, last, there are those who have encountered it before themselves and know of what I speak. Their faces say *OMG YOU ARE RIGHT IT IS ALL UTTERLY INSANE.*

The short version is that we had to treat bats (and newts, but it's best if you don't get me started on the newts) as if they are descended from the Gods, while shelling out obscene amounts of money in ecological surveys, Natural England licence applications and so on, just to be allowed to do up our own home. Money is a vulgar subject, so I shan't say exactly how much, but I have worked out that to cover the costs, I require the editor of *The House* magazine to commission these columns until some date in 2038. (That last sentence is a conservative estimate, not a joke.)

With my homeowner hat on, this stuff drove me to despair. 'The bats were here before you were,' I was told at one point. To which the only reply was: 'But they don't pay the mortgage, do they?'

Yet with my academic hat on, I saw it as a good example of how policy is made. You start with what seems a reasonable set of goals – in this case, to protect wildlife – and that grows, through assorted pieces of legislation and regulation, overseen by largely unaccountable regulatory bodies, into something which I suspect bears little resemblance to what was originally intended. It will form a central part of what is yet another entry in the long list of my unwritten books: *Batshit Crazy: The Unintended Consequences of Well-Meaning Laws.*

One reason why the book may well remain unwritten is just that it would have to roam so widely – in terms of both examples and explanations. Just as a starter, take, for example, the work of the historian Oliver MacDonagh.

In an article published in the very first issue of the *Historical Journal* in 1958, MacDonagh outlined the process by which British government developed in the nineteenth century. First, there was the exposure of a social evil and the passing of general legislation to try to deal with it. But then it was discovered that the initial legislation (often, as he put it, 'an amateur expression of good intentions') had had little effect – and what was required were people to enforce the laws. In turn, those people required regulations to enforce. But as they did so, they also became ever-more aware of legislative loopholes, which led to increasing pressure for more legislation and ever-greater regulations, with increasing discretion in how they applied them. Soon, the officers had become far more than just enforcers of rules; they were now the experts in the field, collecting data and pushing for more and more regulations. It all sounds familiar.

And then there are issues about the quality of legislation – on which there just happens to be some excellent new research published in *Statute Law Review*. The researchers went and asked around 600 solicitors, barristers and academic lawyers a series of questions about the quality of law. These are, to adapt the phrase often attributed to Bismark, the people who eat the sausages.

What was especially neat about this piece of work is that as well as asking about the quality of legislation in general, which everyone bitches about, they asked respondents to identify a particular law they had been working with recently and to talk about that, which helped to produce more focused answers.

Unsurprisingly, questions about the quality of law in general produce more negative responses, but the top complaint, whether you were looking at judgements on legislation in general or specific pieces of legislation, was that it was unnecessarily unwieldy and complex. Next came complaints that wording was ambiguous or that too much of the Act was left to be interpreted, either by secondary legislation or other guidance. The three most common perceived causes of problems were that the law was written by people without sufficient expertise in the area, that additional regulations or amendments have cluttered it up and that it was designed primarily for political, not legal, purposes.

The survey was conducted in England only for simplicity, although I'd put a lot of money on these being UK-wide issues. It was carried out in early 2024. Obviously, things will be different now.

Further reading

LSE GV314 group, 'Cobblers: Lawyers' Views on the Quality of Legislation', *Statute Law Review* (2024).

O. MacDonagh, 'The Nineteenth-Century Revolution in Government: A Reappraisal', *Historical Journal* (1958).

CHAPTER 47

MAJORITIES

'We've got a massive majority.'

At least that's what I heard Keir Starmer say at Prime Minister's Questions on 22 January 2025 – although, for some reason, Hansard records it as: 'We have [*sic*] massive majority.'

Whatever the exact words, how massive?

You're an informed reader, so you don't get any points for knowing the difference between the raw numbers and the actual working majority, once you factor in the non-voting Speaker and his deputies plus the non-sitting Sinn Féin MPs. At the time of writing, the government's working majority in the Commons is 163.

That's lower than it was just after the 2024 election, but whereas the value of your investments may go down as well as up, majorities usually just go down – and anyway, it's still larger than the majorities enjoyed by every single post-war Prime Minister except Tony Blair's first two parliaments between 1997 and 2005. Massive indeed.

But here's a tougher question: how big has the government's majority been in actual votes in the House of Commons since the election?

It varies, of course, from day to day and division to division – but in the first ninety-one whipped votes of this parliament, the government's majority in the Commons averaged a whopping 238. It's even more massive in reality than it seems on paper.

Compare it with the early days of the Blair administration. The average majority in the equivalent first ninety-one whipped votes then was 214. Even though the Blair administration had a slightly larger majority on paper, its majority in practice was slightly smaller than today.

There are several reasons for this, but a key part of the explanation is to be found across the aisle from the government. One of the slightly under-remarked features of the 2024 election is how fragmented the opposition benches are in the Commons. The 121 Conservative MPs elected in 2024 constituted a record low for the party, dating back to 1832. They were elected alongside a total of 117 other opposition MPs who were not Conservative. This is a post-war record. After the election, the Conservatives made up only the narrowest majority (51 per cent) of the opposition.

Compare that to 1997. There were then seventy-five non-Conservative opposition MPs and 165 Tories. In 2001, the figures were eighty and 166 respectively. And in 2005 – which until this election held the post-war record for the parliament with the largest number of MPs not from the two main parties – there were ninety-two compared to 198 Conservatives. In other words, the main opposition party then outnumbered other opposition MPs by 2:1. It's now about 50/50.

Another way of looking at this is to employ a measure called the Effective Number of Parties. This has been used by political scientists to measure the fragmentation of a party system ever since it was first created in 1979.

To calculate it, you divide one by the sum of the squared proportions of the vote or seats gained by each party. This is easier in practice than it sounds when described in the abstract. If Labour had, say, 40 per cent of the votes, the Conservatives 50 per cent and the Lib Dems 10 per cent, you would square each of .4, .5 and .1 (producing: 0.16, 0.25 and 0.01), add the resulting figures together (0.42) and then divide one by that total (1/0.42=2.38).

This produces a measure of party fragmentation, taking into account both how many parties there are and crucially – because this is one of those areas of life where size really does matter – how large they are.

Traditionally, ENP has been applied to votes (the Effective Number of Electoral Parties) or to seats (the Effective Number of Parliamentary Parties). It will surprise no one reading this to discover that the former has risen in Britain dramatically over recent decades, the latter less so. Indeed, 2024 saw the highest ENEP score since universal suffrage, yet the ENPP score actually fell slightly and is about the same now as it was fifty years ago.

But if we look just at the opposition and create an Effective

Number of Opposition Parliamentary Parties (ENOPP) score, then this leapt up in 2024. In the whole of the post-war period, this has varied at Westminster between 1.00 and 1.99. The figure for 2024 was 2.82.

This has several consequences, most obviously when it comes to voting – because it is difficult to find issues around which the varied interests and beliefs of the fragmented opposition parties will coalesce. This has long been true – it's why de facto government majorities are often larger than *de jure* ones – but the more fragmented the opposition, the harder it becomes and the easier life is for the government.

Take the two largest opposition parties – the Conservatives and the Lib Dems – and examine those first ninety or so votes. They were only in the same division lobbies in marginally over a third (35 per cent) of votes.

We might well expect those numbers to change over time. The Lib Dems became increasingly hostile to Labour after 1997 and the same might happen again. But even when they do vote together, there is no guarantee that every other opposition party joins them.

And remember that for the government to get into serious trouble in the division lobbies requires more than just the opposition to be united. That is a necessary but not sufficient condition. It *also* requires a significant number of Labour MPs to defy the whip. It requires an issue which somehow unites the Conservatives, the Lib Dems, Reform UK, the Greens, the independents, the Northern Irish parties *and* a decent chunk of Labour MPs.

Such moments will occasionally happen. One year in and the stars seemed briefly to align over welfare reform, but then the government gave ground, many Labour MPs came back onside and the government won the vote comfortably enough. There may be similar votes to come, but they will not be plentiful – and on more mundane day-to-day issues, the run-of-the-mill stuff that makes government function, Labour enjoys an even larger majority than it appears to have on paper.

Further reading

M. Laaskso and R. Taagepera, '"Effective" Number of Parties: A Measure with Application to Western Europe', *Comparative Political Studies* (1979).

CHAPTER 48

APPS

Several general elections ago, someone created an app to help guide your vote. You told it what you thought on a range of issues and it told you which party you were closest to. Turned out that if you answered 'don't know' to every question, it advised you to vote Lib Dem. You can decide whether this was an example of bias, or a bug or whether it was in fact functioning perfectly.

At the time it was a bit of a novelty, but since then there has been a proliferation in what are called voting advice applications, both in the UK and elsewhere. Given basic coding skills, they are relatively easy to produce. Alas, they are less easy to produce well.

It's easy to understand the appeal. Our democratic ideal might involve a rational man or woman, sitting at home with the party manifestos spread in front of them, a good cup of tea in their hand, ploughing through pages of policy, cogitating deeply and working out which political party they agree with the most before then voting accordingly. The very earliest election studies confirmed what anyone with an understanding of human nature would have long suspected: that voter does not exist. Many votes are cast in ignorance or confusion. Elections are complicated. An app that could cut through the fog and help electors out sounds like a good thing. Voting? There's an app for that.

Although the details vary hugely, most of these apps work by finding out where the voter stands on a range of issues and then calculating which party or candidate they align with the most. The fundamental problem here is not just that we know that this is not how people vote – because you might fairly respond that it would be good if it were and that these apps could help facilitate that. The fundamental problem is that this is not how elections *should* function: that elections are not, and should not be, just about aggregating the policy preferences of voters.

Take, for example, competence. What if I happen to be close, in policy terms, to party A. But party A have just been in power and have proven, at least to my eyes, to be utterly incompetent, full of crooks and shysters and unable to govern effectively. (Hypothetical example, obviously.) I might well like their policies but have little faith in their ability to deliver. Or maybe I like many of the policies of party A, but I think they are implausible or unaffordable and I don't want to vote for an impractical wish list. My vote for party B, with whom in theory I am less aligned, isn't therefore cast in error or mistaken; it is perfectly rational.

Or maybe party A is just led by someone you think is a

complete tool. Leadership is often discussed as if it is solely a heuristic – an intellectual shortcut that saves voters from having to engage with the more difficult work of learning about policies. But even a very well-informed voter, clued up on all the policy issues, might also fairly consider what they think about the people who are going to have to deliver it. Leadership isn't just a heuristic; it's a fundamental aspect of politics.

And this is before we start to engage with any tactical considerations. Maybe party A is closest to you in policy terms, but they do not have a hope in hell of winning – either nationally or in your constituency. What do you do then? Presumably, you turn to your tactical voting app – although that requires you to be informed enough to know that you need to do that…

Yet for all these caveats, apps like this still have value. Although elections aren't all about policies, it would be strange to think that they shouldn't matter at all. If we view these apps not as telling you how to vote but as something educative, helping to inform voters about where the parties stand, then they seem unobjectionable, potentially even useful.

Even this is much harder than it sounds, though. Because to be educative and useful, they have to be accurate. First, what policies do you ask about? You need a range of issues that are comprehensive but not so many that they exhaust the user. They can't overlook anything important, but equally, they can't give undue weight to any set of issues. The questions need to differentiate the parties – there's no point asking about issues where everyone agrees – and they need to ask about issues in terms that the voters understand but which also capture the complexities of the actual policies that parties have. That last one is especially hard. And there's the issue of how you code up party positions in a way that can be tested and which accurately captures the differences between the parties. That's also much harder than it sounds.

Second, you need to control for what is called salience – how important things are to a voter. Some issues may be important, others trivial. Some may be red lines: 'I just could not support a party that...'

And then, third, there's the fundamental question of how you measure how close each voter is to the party. A simple totalling up of agreement, as some of the more basic apps do, can lead to some very strange results, in which question selection becomes very important – especially if it turns out that multiple questions are in fact tapping into the same basic attitudes.

All these sorts of issues can be overcome, just about. Before the 2024 election, I was involved in helping to launch an app called Vote Compass UK. It was a lot of work, thankfully mostly done by other people. Question selection was a multi-stage process, which took place over months. The app allowed for salience to vary and it was more sophisticated than simply measuring percentage agreement. We were very clear that it was educative and not about telling people how to vote. And if you answered 'don't know' to every question, it did not advise you to vote Lib Dem.

Further reading

C. van der Linden and Y. Dufresne, 'The curse of dimensionality in Voting Advice Applications: reliability and validity in algorithm design', *Journal of Elections, Public Opinion and Parties* (2017).

CHAPTER 49

TEACHING

Every year, while preparing for my student trip to Westminster, I swear it will be the last one I organise. To use a technical term common in political science, it is a Grade-A ballache: a massive calling in of favours, juggling the busy diaries of busy people, the ever-present risk of last-minute cancelations or being bumped from the room and the faff of escorting dozens of undergraduates through security. ('Please don't make a joke about a bomb.')

Yet every year, once it's over, I always find myself reflecting that it is one of the more worthwhile things I do.

Every year, it'll be the last. Every year, it isn't.

Over the past couple of decades, more than 100 MPs and peers have spoken to my students, and in part this is just a huge thank you – both to them and to anyone who has spoken at anything similar. But it's also a call to arms for the idea of trying to teach politics away from the seminar room. There is something invaluable for students to be able to engage directly with the thing they are studying. Imagine being a theology student and being able to ask John the Baptist what he thought he was playing at?

Students get to hear someone who 'does' politics; they get real-world examples in which to locate more theoretical material; even when the material delivered by any speakers is essentially the same as that conveyed by academic staff, it can have reinforcement value; and often the talks provide insights and perspectives not available in the classroom or in the academic literature.

Perhaps the exemplar was one student who had often struggled to accept a point I had made to him about the way the Whips' Office functioned; when a Labour Chief Whip made exactly the same point to him, he suddenly got it and the lightbulb went on.

It's also always good to see students have their preconceptions about people challenged. I am especially thinking of the time Michael Gove had an entire room eating out of his hand by the end of the session. And sometimes it's just more *fun*. Seeing students encounter the late Eric Forth was always a highlight. Most politicians take the polite approach to student queries, responding 'that's a very good question' even when it patently isn't; Eric was usually blunter.

There is also benefit in giving students the skills to compete in the political workplace. That's partly about knowledge, but it's much more about the deeper understanding and the softer skills – confidence, especially – that also come from these sorts of interactions.

Ditto for internships or similar schemes which allow students to spend time working in Parliament. These too can be a ball-ache. Demand (from students) always outstrips supply (from MPs). Every election sees some regular host MPs depart, while newcomers must be cajoled to take a student. Having a student in their offices is not always an unalloyed benefit for an MP. Security clearance, alas, has also got harder in recent years.

Placements can vary – one year, one semester, full-time, part-time – but they are all valuable. The effect on students is visible. And again, it's not about knowledge but the softer skills. Those who spend time at Westminster stand taller. This is especially the case for those who perhaps don't come with ambition or confidence already baked in by their background. Not every student who goes on placement loves it, or indeed always wants to work at Westminster later, but it changes almost all of them for the better and plenty do continue in politics. It's how you can tell the age of a politics professor: as they mature, their former students begin to become MPs. They know they are really old when their former students enter the House of Lords.

Queen Mary is one of twenty or so British universities that teach a parliamentary studies module in formal conjunction with Parliament. The implicit assumption underpinning the module is that if we educate people about how their legislature functions, we will increase their faith in it. After all, no one promotes outreach work by institutions in order to diminish faith in them.

Yet it's perfectly plausible to construct a less positive hypothesis: that with knowledge could come negativity. There are plenty of things wrong with most parliaments (and as even its defenders accept, the Westminster one is no exception); bringing these to the attention of students could have entirely the opposite effect to that assumed. This may be one of those occasions when ignorance is, if not bliss, at least preferable.

I bring good news. When this was tested, several years ago, the opposite seemed to be the case. Students who took the module became more knowledgeable about the institution and became more positive both about Parliament and parliamentarians.

Asked a series of factual questions about Westminster, there were increases in knowledge after eight weeks of teaching, ranging from 6 percentage points up to 63. We'd have been worried if teaching hadn't produced an increase in knowledge – although in some of my classes, I do occasionally wonder – but what was more interesting were the changes in attitudes.

The module is taught in a warts-and-all way. Plus, the initial survey had revealed that the student group was much more trusting about and satisfied with Parliament than the general population before the teaching began. Yet even starting from this already high base level, and even though the module involved plenty of the criticisms that are made of Westminster, all three measures of trust and satisfaction improved over the semester, with the question about satisfaction with MPs in general showing the most improvement. Something similar is true of citizenship education in schools. We are saving democracy, one student group at a time.

Further reading

P. Cowley and M. Stuart, 'The Effect of Teaching Parliamentary Studies on Students' Knowledge and Attitudes: A Pilot Study', *Politics* (2015).

J. Tonge et al., 'Does Citizenship Education Make Young People Better-Engaged Citizens?', *Political Studies* (2012).

CHAPTER 50

QUOTES

Almost all the best political quotations – and perhaps the best quotes in general – are not accurate. All half-decent pedants know that no one in *Casablanca* says 'Play it again, Sam', that James Cagney didn't say 'You dirty rat' and that Sherlock Holmes did not announce that things were 'Elementary, my dear Watson' until Basil Rathbone began to play the character in the late 1930s.

Paul Boller and John George's excellent *They Never Said It* claims that a host of political quotes are similarly invented. Among many others, Hermann Göring never said 'Whenever I hear the word culture, I reach for my revolver' (it comes from a 1933 play), Lenin didn't use the phrase 'useful idiots' and Lincoln might have thought that you could fool all the people some of the time and some of the people all the time but not all the people all the time, but he never said it. Similarly, Louis XIV never said 'I am the state' (even if he thought it) and Marie Antoinette never said 'Let them eat cake'. Voltaire never said 'I disapprove of what you say, but I will defend to the death your right to say it'; George Washington never claimed that he couldn't tell a lie.

There's plenty of British examples too. The classic British one is that Jim Callaghan never said 'Crisis, what crisis?' Flying back from the four-nation summit in Guadeloupe in 1979, he was asked by reporters at Heathrow what he thought of 'the mounting chaos in the country at the moment'. He replied: 'I don't think that other people in the world would share the view that there is mounting chaos.' Despite the fact that the word 'crisis' doesn't feature in either the question or the answer, it did in *The Sun*'s headline the following day and 'Crisis, what crisis?' has since become perhaps the most well-known thing Callaghan never said.

Knowing that *The Sun*'s headline wasn't an accurate quote is Political Trivia 101, but you get bonus marks if you knew it was a reference to a line from *The Day of the Jackal* and an album by Supertramp.

The equivalent from the Blair years was that the Labour special adviser Jo Moore never said the words 'bury bad news'. You see it in quotation marks all the time, but although it's a perfectly fair paraphrase, it's not what she wrote. On 11 September 2001, with the world focused on the attacks taking place in the US, she sent an email to her colleagues that said: 'Today is a good day to get out anything we want to bury. Councillors' expenses anyone?' Neither 'bad' nor 'news' (let alone 'bad news') is in there. Yet 'bury bad news' became one of the iconic quotations of the Blair government, despite being as imaginary as Callaghan's 'Crisis, what crisis?'

More recently, we had Liz Truss blaming the 'left-wing economic orthodoxy' for her downfall in an extended essay in the *Sunday Telegraph*. If you've ever met an economist, either an academic one or one working in the City, you'll know they don't, on the whole, lean to the left – and it was taken as a sign of how unmoored from reality some of her views had become. Within days of the article being published, the phrase had made the jump from headlines and articles to memes and gags. The only problem is that she never said it.

The phrase didn't feature once in her almost 4,000-word article. It wasn't even used as the piece's headline – which is where these sorts of problems often start. She did note a leftward shift 'in the media and the wider public sphere' and elsewhere in the article she complained of an 'economic orthodoxy' that was unsympathetic to what she was attempting. The phrase 'left-wing economic orthodoxy' might be considered a fair summary of what she was trying to say – although I don't think it is, because these are two distinct points – and it was used on the paper's front page in their headline. But they didn't put it in quotation marks and nor should we.

For the most part, these quotes survive because they are somehow characteristic of the individuals to whom or time to which they are attributed. Listening to Callaghan's 1979 airport press conference now, it is quite astonishingly complacent in tone. *The Sun* never presented it as a quote; as a headline, it doesn't seem too outrageous. Similarly, 'a good day to bury bad news' is not all that removed from what was in the email and captures well an obsession with media management. (My own view, which is niche, is that Jo Moore was simply doing her job. It was indeed a good day to bury bad news, even if the phrasing was unfortunate.)

And sometimes, these quotes are just very *useful*. In an earlier chapter, I referred to Macmillan's apocryphal response to a journalist asking what was most likely to blow governments off course. He is said to have replied: 'Events, dear boy, events.' (Sometimes, you see it as 'my dear boy', to make it even more in character.) There's no evidence he said it, although he was fond of talking about 'the opposition of events', which is substantively the same point. But if you need a quote to explain the extent to which governments are often derailed by stuff no one saw coming, it's perfect. Shit happens, as Macmillan wouldn't have said.

In other cases, there is no evidence at all for the source. This would apply to the quote about sausages and law referred to in Chapter 46 or the quote about a belief in democracy not surviving an encounter with the average voter in Chapter 19. The former is usually attributed to Bismarck; both have variously been attributed to Churchill, but there's no evidence for either. We could add that Willie Sutton claimed never to have said that he robbed banks because that is where the money is or that there is no evidence that Deep Throat ever said to 'follow the money' (both in Chapter 22); that line was invented for the movie *All the President's Men*. Benjamin Franklin's call to hang together (Chapter 33) is also probably apocryphal.

Real Grade-A pedants won't be worried about things like this, though: they'll all have been too busy googling to prove that the phrase 'Elementary, my dear Watson' began not with Rathbone's performances as Holmes but with the Wodehouse novel *Psmith, Journalist*, published in 1915.

Further reading

P. Boller and J. George, *They Never Said It* (1989).
E. Knowles, *What They Didn't Say* (2006).

ABOUT THE AUTHOR

Philip Cowley is Professor of Politics at Queen Mary University of London. His other books include *The British General Election of 2017*, *The British General Election of 2015* and *The British General Election of 2010* (all written with Dennis Kavanagh), *Sex, Lies and the Ballot Box*, *More Sex, Lies and the Ballot Box*, *Sex, Lies and Politics* (all edited with Robert Ford), *The Rebels*, *Revolts and Rebellions*, *Conscience and Parliament* and three volumes of *Developments in British Politics*.

Philip has lived (in this order) in the following constituencies, a list which, for the most part, shows the growing length and declining utility of their nomenclature: Bristol North East, South Gloucestershire, Northavon, Uxbridge, Hayes and Harlington, Hull North, Selby, Broxtowe, Bermondsey and Old Southwark, Islington South and Finsbury, Vauxhall, Dulwich, Dulwich and West Norwood, Wealdon, and East Grinstead and Uckfield. He has never lived in Scunthorpe.